INDUSTRIEARCHITEKTUR IN EUROPA
INDUSTRIAL ARCHITECTURE IN EUROPE

Katalog/Catalogue
Layout:
Reinhart Wustlich

Übersetzung/Translation:
Renate Vogel
Branco

Auslober/Promoter:
Deutsche Messe AG, Hannover,
in Zusammenarbeit mit,
in conjunction with
Bund Deutscher Architekten BDA,
Bonn/Berlin

Herausgeber/Editors:
Carl Steckeweh, Reinhart Wustlich

Durchführung des Wettbewerbs/
Organization of the competition:
Dipl.-Vw. Carl Steckeweh,
Bund Deutscher Architekten BDA,
Bonn/Berlin

db Verlag DAS BEISPIEL GmbH ©
Darmstadt, 1996
ISBN 3-923974-57-4

Alle Rechte vorbehalten, besonders die der Übersetzung in andere Sprachen. Kein Teil des Buches darf ohne schriftliche Genehmigung des Verlages in irgendeiner Form reproduziert werden.
All rights reserved, especially those of translation into other languages. No part of this publication may be reproduced in any form without written permission of the publisher.

Satz:
Typoservice, Griesheim
Reproduktion:
Grafik Workshop, Pfungstadt
Druck:
Druckhaus Darmstadt, Darmstadt

Ausstellung/Exhibition
Layout:
Reinhart Wustlich

Peter Linden
Olaf Eichbaum

Digitale Bildbearbeitung:
Peter Linden

Digitaldruck:
system repro GmbH, Siegburg

INDUSTRIEARCHITEKTUR IN EUROPA
INDUSTRIAL ARCHITECTURE IN EUROPE

CONSTRUCTEC-PREIS 1996
Europäischer Preis für Industriearchitektur

CONSTRUCTEC PRIZE 1996
European Prize for Industrial Architecture

Reinhart Wustlich
unter Mitarbeit von / in collaboration with
Carl Steckeweh
im Auftrag / commissioned by
Deutsche Messe AG, Hannover
Bund Deutscher Architekten BDA, Bonn/Berlin

db Verlag Das Beispiel GmbH, Darmstadt

Inhalt/Contents

6 Sepp D. Heckmann **Vorwort** — **Preface**

8 Andreas Gottlieb Hempel
Die Zukunft hat schon begonnen — **The future has already begun**

11 Reinhart Wustlich
Megalopolis – Technopolis
Technologiewandel und Raumanspruch im Ruhrgebiet

Megalopolis – Technopolis Technological change and the right to space in the Ruhr

33 **CONSTRUCTEC-PREIS 1996** Ziele, Themen und Teilnahmebereich, Jury

CONSTRUCTEC PRIZE 1996 Targets, themes and eligibility, Jury

CONSTRUCTEC-PREIS 1996
Besondere Auszeichnungen

CONSTRUCTEC PRIZE 1996
Special Awards

39 **CONSTRUCTEC-PREIS 1996**
EMPA – Eidgenössische Materialprüf- und Forschungsanstalt, St. Gallen (CH), ABB Kraftwerke AG Engineering, Forschung und Entwicklung, Baden (CH), Betriebsgebäude Gaswerkareal – Städtische Werke Winterthur (CH)

CONSTRUCTEC PRIZE 1996
Theo Hotz, Architekt/Architect, Zürich/Zurich (CH)

CONSTRUCTEC-AUSZEICHNUNGEN 1996

CONSTRUCTEC AWARDS 1996
Award Winners

57 **Gebäude für Lager-Technik, Wolfurt** Building Store-Technology, Wolfurt (A)

Architekten/Architects:
C. Baumschlager & D. Eberle, Lochau (A)

65 Uhrenfabrik Corum, **La Chaux-de-Fonds** Clock Manufacturing Plant Corum, La Chaux-de-Fonds (CH)	Architekten/Architects: **M. Althammer + R. Hochuli,** Zürich/Zurich (CH)
73 SBB-Stellwerk, Basel SBB Signal Box, Basel (CH)	Architekten/Architects: **Herzog & de Meuron,** Basel (CH)
81 Wasseraufbereitungsanlage **Sagep, Paris** Water Purification Plant Sagep, Paris (F)	Architekt/Architect: **Dominique Perrault,** Paris (F)
89 Zentrum zur Erforschung **humaner Arzneimittel, Leiden** Research Centre Human Pharmaceutics, Leiden (NL)	Architekten/Architects: **CEPEZED**/BV, Delft (NL)
97 Institut für angewandte Mikro- **elektronik, Braunschweig** Institute of Micro-Electronics, Braunschweig (D)	Architekten/Architects: **Schulitz + Partner,** Braunschweig (D)
105 Hallenneubau A. & C. Wallner, **Scheifling** Workshop A. & C. Wallner, Scheifling (A)	Architekt/Architect: **Andreas Ortner,** Graz (A)
113 Inelcom-Werk, Valencia Inelcom Plant, Valencia (E)	Architekt/Architect: **Arturo Sanz, ACME,** Valencia (E)
122 Reinhart Wustlich **Technik und Arbeit – eine Episode**	**Technology and work – an episode**

Sepp D. Heckmann

VORWORT

Innovationen im Industriebau – diese Thematik genießt höchste Aufmerksamkeit im Rahmen der Internationalen Fachmesse für Technische Gebäudesysteme, Bautechnik und Architektur, der CONSTRUCTEC HANNOVER. Es ist unser Ziel, diese Innovationen der Öffentlichkeit zu präsentieren und die Aufmerksamkeit eines hochrangigen Fachpublikums auf kreative Planungsideen, neue Technologien und beispielhafte Kooperationen zu lenken. Mit der Auslobung des CONSTRUCTEC-Preises für Industriebau ist es gelungen, ein Instrument zu entwickeln, das nicht nur herausragende Objekte selbst würdigt, sondern vor allem die Zusammenarbeit zwischen den Architekten, Ingenieuren, Bauherren und Investoren.

Der CONSTRUCTEC-Preis wurde 1996 zum zweiten Mal gemeinsam mit dem Bund Deutscher Architekten BDA ausgelobt. Diese Zusammenarbeit hat sich bereits zur vergangenen Veranstaltung bestens bewährt und zu hervorragenden Ergebnissen geführt. 1996 wurden insgesamt 49 Objekte aus zehn Nationen eingereicht. Es beteiligten sich 36 Büros aus Belgien, Italien, Großbritannien, den Niederlanden, Österreich, der Schweiz, Spanien, Tschechien, Japan und Deutschland. Diese erfreuliche Beteiligung aus Europa und Asien ist ein Beleg für das große kreative Potential internationaler Architekturbüros und den hohen Stellenwert moderner Industriearchitektur.

Das neunköpfige Expertenteam aus Dänemark, den Niederlanden und Deutschland hat es sich bei der Auswahl der zu prämiierenden Arbeiten nicht leichtgemacht. Gleich drei Objekte wurden aufgrund ihrer außergewöhnlichen Qualität ausgezeichnet. Gelobt wurden bei den Bauten des Schweizers Theo Hotz, dem CONSTRUCTEC-Preisträger 1996, vor allem „die ganzheitlichen Planungsansätze und die integrierte Planung, die zu einer Minimierung

PREFACE

Innovations in industrial construction are always a key topic at CONSTRUCTEC HANNOVER, the international trade fair for building services, construction and architecture. It is our goal to present these innovations to the general public and to focus the attention of the top trade professionals on creative planning ideas, new technologies and exemplary cooperative undertakings. We have been successful in developing the CONSTRUCTEC Award for industrial construction as an instrument which honours not only outstanding objects, but also the cooperative efforts made by architects, engineers, building owners and investors working together.

In cooperation with the Bund Deutscher Architekten BDA, Bonn/Berlin, we will be presenting the CONSTRUCTEC Award for the second time in 1996. This collaboration already proved very successful at the last event and produced excellent results. In 1996, a total of 49 objects were submitted from ten different countries. 36 offices from Belgium, Italy, Great Britain, the Netherlands, Austria, Switzerland, Spain, the Czech Republic, Japan and Germany entered into the competition. This high rate of participation from Asia as well as Europe is proof positive of the great creative potential of international architecture agencies and the high status of modern industrial architecture.

It was no simple task for the team of nine experts from Denmark, the Netherlands and Germany to select the prize-winning entries. No less than three objects received an award for their exceptional quality. The buildings designed by Switzerland's Theo Hotz, recipient of the 1996 CONSTRUCTEC Award, were commended particularly for "the interdisciplinary approaches to planning and the integrated planning procedures which reduce technical requirements and energy costs to a minimum".

des technischen Ausbaus sowie der Energiekosten führten". Dieser ganzheitliche und integrale Ansatz verdeutlicht das Konzept der CONSTRUCTEC HANNOVER, die mit ihrem Systemcharakter die am Bau beteiligten Partner einander näherbringt und zum interdisziplinären Dialog aufruft.

Nicht nur die drei Objekte aus der Schweiz, auch die weiteren acht Arbeiten, die mit besonderen Auszeichnungen versehen wurden, stellen herausragende Leistungen auf dem Gebiet des Industriebaus dar. Es freut uns, allen ausgezeichneten Objekten eine gemeinsame Plattform anzubieten, die der modernen Industriearchitektur einen idealen Rahmen gibt und sie noch stärker ins Blickfeld der Öffentlichkeit rückt. Wir möchten uns ganz herzlich für das große Engagement aller Teilnehmer und die hohe Qualität der eingereichten Arbeiten bedanken, welche die gesamte Jury beeindruckten. Wir freuen uns auf eine interessante Ausstellung während der CONSTRUCTEC '96.

Sepp D. Heckmann
Mitglied des Vorstandes, Deutschen Messe AG, Hannover

This interdisciplinary and integrated approach clearly reflects the CONSTRUCTEC HANNOVER concept, which uses its emphasis on systems to draw partners in the building process closer together and to stimulate interdisciplinary dialogue.

Not only the three objects from Switzerland, but also the other eight works which received special awards, represent outstanding achievements in the field of industrial construction. We are pleased to offer all of the prizewinning entries a common platform, which provides modern industrial architecture with an ideal backdrop and places them in the public eye. We would like to express our most sincere thanks to all of the participants for their hard work. The high quality of their entries made a strong impression on the entire jury. We look forward to an interesting exhibition at the CONSTRUCTEC '96 show.

Sepp D. Heckmann
Member of the Deutsche Messe AG Board of Directors, Hannover

Andreas Gottlieb Hempel   **DIE ZUKUNFT HAT SCHON BEGONNEN**   **THE FUTURE HAS ALREADY BEGUN**

Die große Masse der Bauten in der Bundesrepublik Deutschland entsteht derzeit weitgehend unter den ökonomischen Gesetzen des Marktes. Das Interesse an einer neu verstandenen Qualität gebauter Umwelt ist zwar vorhanden, findet aber in der Realität wenig Niederschlag. Allenfalls ist Gestaltqualität ein Faktor, der weithin verstanden wird, häufig aber als überflüssiger Luxus gilt, wenn sie sich nicht ebenfalls als Corporate identity vermarkten läßt.

An der Schwelle zum Dritten Jahrtausend empfinden wir Qualitätskriterien für das Bauen – vor allem für die sogenannte Alltagsarchitektur – als immer dringlicher, wenn wir ein ökologisches und soziales Desaster vermeiden wollen: Schonung der Ressourcen, Kreislaufwirtschaft, Umweltqualität usw. Kurzum: Wandel ohne Wachstum muß das Ziel sein. Gestaltqualität kann künftig nicht nur das Erscheinungsbild als „Fassade" betreffen, sondern muß aus neuen Strukturen, welche die genannten und weitere Kriterien umfassen, entwickelt werden. Vieles, was uns heute an neuer Architektur geboten wird, ist möglicherweise gestalterisch interessant, strukturell aber längst veraltet.

Der Industriebau hat in der Architektur schon immer eine Sonderrolle eingenommen. Abseits gerade gängiger Gestaltungsmoden richtet sich die Gestaltqualität von Industriebauten mehr nach den Vorgaben der Fertigung, der Betriebsabläufe und anderen Funktionen der Nutzung.

Deshalb kann auch heute wieder beobachtet werden, daß tiefgreifende architektonische Innovationen vor allem vom Industriebau ausgehen. Es werden neue Techniken, vor allem auch Umwelttechniken erprobt; hier treten sie in der Gestalt der Gebäude als neue Formen in Erscheinung – vorausgesetzt, engagierte Archi-

Most of the buildings constructed in the Federal Republic of Germany are still to a large extent subject to the economic rules of the market. Interest in a newly understood quality of the built environment does exist though, but leaves few traces in reality. Quality of design is at best a factor which meets with broad acceptance, but is often regarded as a superfluous luxury unless marketable as corporate identy.

On the threshold into the third millenium, we recognize that further building criteria – particularly for socalled every-day architecture – are more and more urgent in order to avoid an ecological and social disaster: resource-savings, an economy based on recycling, environment quality etc., in short the goal must be a change without growth.

In future, design quality cannot only manifest itself in terms of "façades", but must be developed out of new structures comprising the said and other criteria. Much of what is today offered as new architecture is possibly interesting from a design-point-of-view, but long since obsolete as far as the structure is concerned.

Industrial building has always played a special role in architecture. Off the beaten track of habitual design fashions, the design quality of industrial buildings rather adjusts to the requirements of production, operational procedures and other functions of utilisation.

This is the reason why today profound architectural innovations can in particular be observed in the field of industrial architecture. New techniques, especially environmental techniques, are being tested, and appear as a new form in the shape of buildings – provided a highly motivated architect does his best to creatively implement functional and structural data.

tekten bemühen sich, die funktionellen und strukturellen Vorgaben gestalterisch umzusetzen.

Insofern kommt dem CONSTRUCTEC-Preis, der alle zwei Jahre verliehen wird, eine besondere Bedeutung zu. Neue architektonische Entwicklungen auf neuen technischen Vorgaben können auf ihre Logik und Konsequenz überprüft werden. Aus diesem Grund hat sich die Jury 1996 entschlossen, die Arbeiten des Schweizer Architekten Theo Hotz besonders herauszustellen: Bei ihm erscheinen neue Architekturformen begründet aus der konsequenten Umsetzung neuer technischer Entwicklungen. Sie sind aus ökologischen, energetischen und arbeitstechnischen Anforderungen abgeleitet.

Der Deutschen Messe AG Hannover gilt erneut besonderer Dank für die Auslobung des CONSTRUCTEC-Preises, zu dem 1996 neunundvierzig Objekte aus zehn Nationen eingereicht wurden – man kann wohl sagen, es waren die Besten der Besten.

Dipl.-Ing. Andreas Gottlieb Hempel, München
Präsident des Bundes Deutscher Architekten BDA

Insofar, the bi-annually awarded CONSTRUCTEC-Prize has a special significance. Recent architectural developments based on new technical data can be examined with regard to their logic and consequences. This is why in 1996 the Jury decided the expressly highlight on the works of the Swiss Architect Theo Hotz: New architectural forms emerge from his works, based on his persistently implementing new technical developments derived from ecological, energetic and technical requirements.

Special thanks to the Deutsche Messe AG Hannover for organizing the CONSTRUCTEC-Prize for which in 1996 were received 49 submissions from ten countries. I believe these were the best of the best.

Dipl.-Ing. Andreas Gottlieb Hempel, Munich
President of the Bund Deutscher Architekten BDA

MEGALOPOLIS – TECHNOPOLIS
Technological change and the right to space in the Ruhr

Reinhart Wustlich

Megalopolis – unknown One of the gigantic cities in Europe which is most interesting on account of the change it is going through is called, in German, the Ruhrgebiet, or simply "the Ruhr" – the mass of cities along the river of that name. One of the structural characteristics dominating the appearance of this huge urban landscape is the relationship, founded in the situation of the 19th century, between technology and the right to space to live in. As the heavy industries of coal and steel came to be founded, and then to develop their own identities, infrastructural networks arose which embraced them all. A wickerwork of cities and links between them characterises this area, which is closer to the image of urban regions all over the world than to any idea of compactness and urban orderliness. At one point you will find the neat and tidy city centre, next the airy suburbs, then the historically embedded and jointed structure of the centre, ideologically obsolete, and then again the edge of the Ruhr, thinly populated in places, accessible, but under-represented in city memories.

The technological change overcoming the highly detailed forms of civilisation has shown, in the image of change in this and comparable regions, that technology is not free of geographical resources but must be thought of in terms of the claim it makes to living-space. The claim made by this megalopolis had the result that "in historical development, the individual construction project was forced further and further into the background" (Karl Ganser) and these all-embracing factors dominated the outward appearance.

The north part of the Ruhr, the area around the IBA International Building Exhibition in Emscher Park, stretches out over an urban and industrial region 70 kilometres long and 15 wide. The total area of the Ruhr, including the

Pavillon der Emschergenossenschaft/ Emscher pavilion, Bottrop; Architekten/ architects: Hansen + Petersen, Dortmund

Fotos: Reinhart Wustlich

Die Technopolis des Ruhrgebiets im Technologiewandel und im Wandel des Raumanspruchs: Kokerei der Zeche Prosper, Bottrop; oben: Hochöfen des stillgelegten Hüttenwerks der Thyssen Stahl AG – nun Landschaftspark Duisburg-Nord/ Technopolis of the Ruhr - changing technology and different claim to space: cokery of the Prosper colliery, Bottrop; above: old kilns of the iron smelting works abandoned by Thyssen Stahl AG, now Landscape park Duisburg-Nord

schenzeitlich reformierten Gemeindegrenzen nicht mit dem Revier, sondern mit sich selbst identisch sein wollen: Essen, Bochum, Oberhausen, Dortmund.

Ein kurzer Blick auf Regionen, die einen vergleichbar aufregenden Strukturwandel durchmachen, zeigt Rotterdam in der „Randstad" der Niederlande – mit der Ausdehnung einer Hafenstadtregion von 40 Kilometern Länge, in deren Osten an Hafen- und Infrastrukturflächen brachgefallen ist, wofür im Westen bis Maasvlakte auf neuer technologischer Stufe die Entwicklung vorbereitet und strukturiert wurde. Kop van Zuid etwa blieb als zentrumsnahes Entwicklungsgebiet zurück, die Hafeneinrichtungen und ihre begleitenden Industrien wanderten nach Westen zur Küste aus.

Die Berliner Stadtregion, sie mißt von Falkensee im Westen bis Hoppegarten im Osten ebenfalls 40 Kilometer, zeigt einen anderen Weg, Technologiewandel und Raumanspruch in ein neues Verhältnis zu setzen. Daß dabei die Prinzipien und Strukturen der Stadt des 19. Jahrhunderts wiederentdeckt werden, erscheint paradox genug. Paradox genug, um darauf hinzuweisen, daß die Standortprobleme, die im Ruhrgebiet, insonderheit mit den Projekten der IBA Emscher Park mit enormem Aufwand kompensiert werden, Folgen des Technologiewandels des 19. und frühen 20. Jahrhunderts sind, deren Raumanspruch nun revidiert wird.

Revision des technischen Raumanspruchs Die Entwicklung einer Megalopole, die sich aus dem historisch begründeten Verhältnis von Technologiewandel und Raumanspruch lösen will, wäre umgekehrt zu befragen: Nach welchen geänderten Kategorien ist dieser Raumanspruch zu bestimmen – und welche Technologien sind unter diesen korrigierten

places in which it historically originated, is twice as deep. As a "megalopolis" it is therefore unknown, because its urban cells with their municipal borders, historically established but now reformed, are trying to identify not with the Ruhr as a whole but with themselves: Essen, Bochum, Oberhausen, Dortmund.

A brief glimpse at regions which are undergoing a similarly exciting period of structural change will include Rotterdam in the "Randstad" – the conglomeration of merging cities – of Holland, forming a port city and hinterland region 40 kilometres long, with its eastern part, port, and infrastructural areas falling into decay, whereas in the west, as far across as Maasvlakte, development is being prepared and structured on a new, technological level. Kop van Zuid might be described as having been left behind as a central development area.

The Berlin urban region, measured from Falkensee in the west to Hoppegarten in the east and likewise 40 kilometres across, shows a different way of establishing a new relationship between technological change and the right to living-space. It is enough of a paradox that this led to a rediscovery of the principles and structures of the city in the 19th century – so much so that it demonstrates that the location problems compensated for in the Ruhr particularly in the IBA Emscher Park projects at such enormous expense were the consequences of the technological change that took place at the end of the 19th century and the beginning of the 20th, and their claim to living-space is now subject to review.

Review of technology's claim to living-space The development of a megalopolis which is trying to divorce itself from the historically established relationship between

Rahmenbedingungen geeignet, den Strukturwandel der Stadt zu erfüllen?

Im Katalog zur VI. Architektur Biennale, „Wandel ohne Wachstum", schreibt Karl Ganser, die Entwicklungsstrategie im nördlichen Ruhrgebiet sei die der „Konkretisierung und der Annäherung an die globale Forderung einer ‚nachhaltigen Entwicklung'", deren Basiselemente seien:
- kein weiterer Flächenverbrauch, sondern Übergang zur Kreislaufwirtschaft in der Flächennutzung;
- Verlängerung der Nutzungsdauer von Gebäuden und Produktionsanlagen durch Instandhaltung, Modernisierung und Umnutzung; Neubau nur nach den Prinzipien des ökologischen Bauens;
- Transformation der Produktionsstruktur in der Region hin zu ökologisch verträglichen Produkten und Produktionsverfahren[1].

So wird der Hintergrund beschrieben, der das einzelne Bauvorhaben in seine übergreifende Perspektive integriert. Im Längsschnitt der Entwicklung treten die Prinzipien des Technologiewandels hervor, für den Bauwerke die erfahrbaren Zeichen sind.

Ökologische Erneuerung bedeutet Wandel von einer schweren, raumbeanspruchenden Generationen von Technik zu einer leichten, technischen Ökologie des Bauens, die mit dem Raum in einem ursprünglicheren Wortsinn kultiviert umgeht. Das aus der gleichen Wurzel abgeleitete Wort Kultur kam im ursprünglichen Wortsinn von cultivare = pflegen, vom pfleglichen Umgang mit Natur und Siedlung. Pfleglicher Umgang hieß, die Zukunft einzubeziehen. Cultivare heißt heute: Einhalt gebieten im Sinne nachhaltiger Rücksichtnahme, heißt: hinzufügen, ergänzen.

Das Cultivare einer anders verstandenen Baukultur bedeutete dann, das Bauen auf frei-

changing technology and the claim to living-space could be faced with the question in reverse: by what changed categories is this claim to living-space to be determined, and what technologies are suitable, under these revised outline conditions, to fulfil the structural change of the city?

In the catalogue of the VI. Architectural Biennale, "Change without Growth", Karl Ganser writes that the development strategy in the northern part of the Ruhr is that of the "itemisation and approximation to the global demand for 'permanent development'", the bases of which are, in his view:
- no further consumption of land, but a transition to the closed-circuit economy in the usage of land;
- prolongation of the service life of buildings and factories through maintenance, modernisation, and conversion, with any new buildings adhering to the principles of ecological construction;
- transformation of the production structure in the region in favour of ecologically compatible products and production processes.[1]

This is how the background is described which integrates the individual construction project into its surrounding perspective. Taking a longitudinal cross-section through the development reveals the principles of technological change for which buildings are the perceptible signs.

Ecological renewal means changing from a heavy generation of technology which took up a lot of space to a light, technical ecology in building, which has a relationship with living-space which is "cultivated" in the original sense of the term. The word culture, which stems from the same root, originally came from cultivare, to till and tend a garden or a field, and indicates a "cultured" way of dealing with

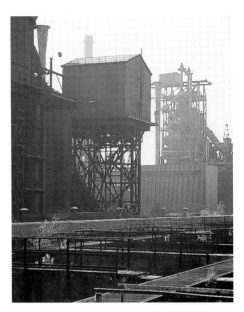

Ökologische Erneuerung: Wandel von einer schweren, raumbeanspruchenden Generation von Technik zu einer leichten, technischen Ökologie/
Ecological renewal: changing from a heavy generation of technology which took up a lot of space to a light, technical ecology

Technische Kontradiktion: während der technische Sektor seit dem 19. Jahrhundert auf der behaupteten „Fortschrittlichkeit" der Entwicklung beharrte, zeigen die Reaktivierungsanstrengungen, daß Modernisierung eine Kompensation von Technikfolgen bedeutet/
Technical contradiction: the technical sector insisting ever since the 19th century on the "progressiveness" of development, but the subsequent modernisation now signifies principally an expensive removal for technological consequences

gesetzten Arealen leichter, strukturell durchdachter, materialsparender und transparenter zu machen – und zugleich dem ehemals überformten Land zurückzugeben, was so nicht weiter beansprucht werden muß: freie Flächen zur naturnäheren Regeneration. Verlängerung der Nutzungsdauer heißt: das Gebäude als transfunktionelles Projekt zu verstehen, es von einem eingeengten Funktionsbegriff abzulösen.

Eine der interessantesten Positionen, die Gesellschaftstheorie und das Projekt zu verbinden, bezieht sich auf Henri Lefèbvres Einschätzung, weder die vergängliche städtebauliche Ordnung des 19. Jahrhunderts noch der chaotische städtebauliche Rahmen der Megalopolen könne zum verbindlichen Gesetz und zum Rahmen des architektonischen Projekts erhoben werden, das die eigene architektonische Entfaltung, quasi von außen, fremdbestimme – oder die Entwicklung seiner Eigenart gar unterbinde. Die Architektur, so der französische Soziologe, sei als Monument transfunktionell, sie könne unterschiedliche Funktionen beherbergen: wie der Ort, an dem sie realisiert werde. Bis zum Augenblick der Realisierung habe Architektur keine eigene Geschichte. Sie habe sich eigene Identität erst zu erwerben, nicht auszuleihen. Und der Kontext, selbst grundlegend wandelbar, sei nicht dazu da, das Projekt zu beherrschen. Zur Projekterfahrung gehört nun, daß eine Generationenfolge von Funktionen ein und desselben Projekts zu seiner Identität beitragen können. Und daß zu dieser Identität eine entspannte Koexistenz mit dem Freiraum der Stadtlandschaft gehört.

Landschaftsmuseum des heroischen Stahls In Duisburg grenzt an den Stadtteil Meiderich eines der post-industriellen Projekte der durch den Wandel erzwungenen Koexistenz alter Strukturen des Reviers mit der Landschaft:

Nature and human settlements. And this in turn means taking the future into account. Cultivare today means: showing consideration in the sense of permanently respecting, and it means adding and completing. When applied to architecture with a different definition it means putting up buildings on open land which are structurally better thought out, use less materials, and are more transparent, and also to give something back to the once over-tilled land so that it does not have to suffer further harm: open spaces for regeneration close to Nature. Lengthening service life means defining a building as a transfunctional project, releasing it from the definition of a single confining function.

One of the most interesting positions connecting sociological theory with the project relates to Henri Lefèbvre's judgement that neither the transient urban architectural order of the 19th century nor the chaotic urban parameters of the megalopolis could be elevated to the level of binding law or form the framework for the architectonic project which determines one's own architectonic development as if it were formed through an outside factor, and certainly not one which prohibits the development of one's own individual style. Architecture, according to this French sociologist, is as a monument transfunctional, and can accommodate a number of different functions, like the place in which it is built. Until the moment of implementation, architecture has no history of its own. It must first acquire its own identity, not lend it out. And the context, which is itself fundamentally mutable, does not in his view have the purpose of dominating the project. It is in fact part of project experience that a sequence of generations of functions can contribute to the identity of one and the same project, and that part of this identity is a relaxed

Landschaftspark Duisburg-Nord: ein Bereich industriegeschichtlicher Topografie, nun der „Rückeroberung" durch die Natur ausgesetzt/
Landscape park Duisburg-Nord: an area where the topography is steeped in industrial history, now exposed to being "conquered back" by Nature

Landschaftsarchitekten/landscape architects: Peter Latz + Partner, Kranzberg near Munich

der Landschaftspark Duisburg-Nord, ein Bereich industriegeschichtlicher Topografie (Landschaftsarchitekten: Peter Latz + Partner), der auf einer über 200 ha großen Industriebrache des Montanbereichs entsteht.

Das Gelände des 1985 stillgelegten Hüttenwerkes der Thyssen Stahl AG übergreifend, ist ein Landschaftspark entstanden, der einen industriegeschichtlichen Pfad durch eine vergangene techologische Zivilisation legt. Die co-existence with the open spaces in the urban landscape.

The landscape museum of heroic steel

In Duisburg, on the border of a suburb called Meiderich, there is a post-industrial project based on the enforced co-existence of the old structures of the Ruhr with the surrounding landscape: the landscape park of Duisburg-Nord, an area where the topography is steeped

Mauern und Strukturen der früheren Erzbunker des Hüttenwerks, nun Klettergarten des Landschaftsparks Duisburg-Nord/ Walls and structures of the former ore bunker in the iron smelting works, now climber's garden of the Landscape park Duisburg-Nord

Kerne des Hüttenwerks, das zwischen 1902 und 1908 erbaut und in verschiedenen Stufen erneuert wurde, sind als Industriemuseum erhalten. Das Hochofenwerk, dessen Hochofen 5 erst 1973 neu erbaut wurde, produzierte Spezialroheisen, die es als „Apotheke des Ruhrgebiets" bekanntmachten. Trotz der modernen Technik des Werkes erfolgte bereits zwölf Jahre nach der Erneuerung die Stillegung. Das landschaftsplanerische Konzept sieht vor, die Eingriffe des technologischen Raumanspruchs in die Landschaft nicht idyllisch zu überdecken. Es läßt die spontan wachsende Vegetation, die den Standort unmerklich zurückgewinnt, die geordneten Pflanzungen, Wege- und Platzkonzepte, die neuen kulturellen Nutzungen und die Bastionen des Hüttenwerks einander überlagern.

Werke dieser Dimension, ehemalig verbotene Orte mit strengster Zugangskontrolle, sind nun der „Rückeroberung" durch die Natur ausgesetzt – etwas von der Vergeblichkeit wird

in industrial history (the landscape architects were Peter Latz & Partners), a 200 hectare (500 acre) site left derelict by the demise of heavy iron and steel industry.

More than covering the site of an iron smelting works abandoned by Thyssen Stahl AG in 1985, a landscape park is being created which lays a path of industrial history through a vanished technological civilisation. The central core of the smelting works, built between 1902 and 1908 and renovated at various stages, has been retained as an industrial museum. The smelting furnaces, of which Kiln 5 was built new as recently as 1973, used to produce the special raw iron which made it famous as the "chemist's shop of the Ruhr". Despite the modern technology in this factory, it was closed down only 12 years after it had been modernised. The landscape architect's concept does not provide for attacking the technological claim to living-space and covering it over with idyllic perfection, but allows the vegetation that

spürbar, die natürlichen Lebensbedingungen ignorieren zu wollen. Die Säulenbasen der Verladebrücken der ehemaligen Erz- und Zuschlagbunker, heute in einen Klettergarten einbezogen, erinnern mit ihrer vergessenen Schwere an die Dimensionen der Säulengänge des Ramses II. in Luxor: für die „Ewigkeit" gebaut. So sieht ein Ort aus, an dem die Zeit angehalten wird, ein Ort für den nachdenklichen Betrachter.

Baudenkmal als Hallenraum Die großen Backsteinflügel der Zechengebäude Rheinpreussen in Moers aus dem Jahre 1906 wurden dagegen nicht als Nachlaß einer versunkenen Welt aufgegeben, als die Zeche 1989 stillgelegt wurde. In fast fließendem Übergang wurden die Flügel und die Zechenhalle einem Reaktivierungsprozeß unterzogen – Verlängerung der Nutzungsdauer von Gebäuden als konkretes Programm: Modernisierung, Hinzufügung und Technologieaustausch waren die architektonischen Mittel, mit denen Wolfgang Felder, Baucoop, arbeitete. Die Gebäudeteile, etwa der zentrale Flügel der alten Markscheiderei wurden als Hallenräume neu interpretiert. Das entkernte Gebäude wurde bis auf das Tragwerk und die Schichten der begrenzenden Dach- und Wandflächen reduziert und als großer Leerraum erhalten. Die eingestellten Kuben für Büros und Kombibüros: minimalistische Beton'stages', Bühneneinbauten einer neuen Generation von Büros für das Institut für Mechatronik. Technische Lösungen für die Hard- und Software industrieller Steuerungen werden hier entwickelt. Gläserne Dachaufbauten und ein mit Glas aufgestockter Seitenflügel des Bildungszentrums ergänzen den historischen Zechenbau, ohne strukturell in Widerspruch zu geraten. Die Klarheit, die durch den Wandel im Inneren erreicht wird, ist frappierend: das

grows spontaneously to reconquer the site surreptitiously, so that the artificially ordered plantings, paths, and squares, the new cultural uses, and the bastions of the smelting works all overlap one another.

Factories of these dimensions, once prohibited cities with very strict guards at the gates, are now exposed to the danger of being "conquered back" by Nature. It is possible to perceive something of the hopelessness of trying to ignore the natural conditions of life. The plinths of the pillars of the loading bridges of the old ore and slag bunkers, now integrated into a garden of climbing plants, have the forgotten heaviness reminiscent of the lines of columns of Ramses II in Luxor: built "for eternity". This is how a place looks where time has stood still, a place for meditative contemplation.

Memorial as hall The big brick-built wings of the Rheinpreussen colliery building in Moers, built in 1906, on the other hand, were not abandoned as the legacy of a vanished world when the mine was closed down in 1989. The brick wings and the factory building made an almost flowing transition into a re-activation process, prolonging the service life of the buildings as part of a specific programme. Modernisation, addition, and technological transfer were the architectonic means with which Wolfgang Felder, of Baucoop, worked. The main parts of the building such as the central wing of the old separating house were re-interpreted as an open hall. The whole building was gutted down to its structure and the layers of the restricting roof and wall surfaces reduced and retained as a huge, empty space. The former cubes for offices and combi-offices: minimal concrete "stages", stage settings for a new generation of offices for the Institute of

**Zechengebäude Rheinpreussen in Moers: Modernisierung, Hinzufügung, Technologieaustausch/
Rheinpreussen colliery building in Moers: modernisation, addition, technological transfer**

**Architekt/architect: Wolfgang Felder, Baucoop, Köln
Fotos (5): Lukas Roth**

Technik und Natur/Technology and Nature

**Das Gebäude lernt von der Technologie: Historismus und neue Moderne gehen eine Verbindung ein/
The building is learning from technology: Historism and the new modern enter into a combination**

Gebäude lernt von der Technologie. Historismus und neue Moderne gehen eine Verbindung ein, die beide Prinzipien in der Wirkung steigert. Auf dem Boden der Schwerindustrie des 19. Jahrhunderts ist ein modernes Technologiezentrum entstanden, das offen und kommunikativ ist, Schulungseinrichtungen und Forschungsmöglichkeiten enthält.

Technik und Natur Bereits in der Krise der dreißiger Jahre wurden grundlegende Positionen zur Entwicklung von Technik und Gesellschaft erörtert. Versuch einer Vorausschau, die erst mit großer Verspätung zur Geltung gekommen ist – und mit Überlegungen zum gesellschaftlichen Wandel von heute korrespondiert. Norbert Elias' Zivilisationstheorie gehört dazu (1936 geschrieben), welche die langfristigen Transformationen der Gesellschafts- und Persönlichkeitsstrukturen zum Gegenstand hat. Friedrich Georg Jüngers „Perfektion der Technik" gehört dazu (1939 geschrieben, 1946 erst erschienen), welche die langfristigen Transformationen der Technologie und der Persönlichkeitsstrukturen zum Gegenstand hat.

Von der Unabwendbarkeit des technischen Prozesses hat Sigfried Giedion in „Mechanization Takes Command" zwischen 1941 und 1945 berichtet (1948 in den USA, aber erst 1982 in deutscher Sprache erschienen) und dabei das Motiv des unbeobachteten Hervorkommens des Neuen gemeint: die Technik als das auf lange Sicht die Lebensweise Bestimmende wird nie gewollt und geplant, tritt durch eine unbeachtete Pforte ein, hält sich eine Weile verborgen, um schließlich „durch alle Sinne" in das „Innerste der Seele" vorzudringen (Henning Ritter).

Die Doppelgesichtigkeit der Technik hat Jünger beschrieben, wenn er einerseits feststellt: „Die Utopie braucht ein Schema, das

Mechatronics. Technical systems for the hardware and software of industrial control units are developed here. Glass roof structures and a side-wing of the training centre extended upwards in glass complete the historical mine building without falling into a structural contradiction. The clarity attained in the interior by the technological change is awe-inspiring: the building is learning from technology. Historism and the new modern enter into a combination which increases the effect of both principles. On the basis of 19th century heavy industry, a modern technology centre has arisen which is open and communicative, and contains training and research facilities.

Technology and Nature As long ago as the crisis years in the 1930s, fundamental positions were discussed on the development of technology and society. It was an attempt at making a forecast which has only come true after a long delay, and corresponds with considerations concerning the social change of today. Norbert Elias' civilisation theory (written in 1936) is part of this, and concerns itself with the long-term transformation of social and personality structures. Friedrich Georg Jünger's "Perfection of technology" (written in 1939, but not published until 1946) is also part of it, and this likewise concerns itself with the long-term transformation of technology and personality structures.

Sigfried Giedion reported between 1941 and 1945 on the ineluctability of the technical process in "Mechanization takes Command" (published in the USA in 1948, but not published in German until 1982), and this is meant to mean the unnoticed advance of the new; technology in the sense of the factor that determines our way of life is never wanted and never planned, but it enters through an unnoticed

einer rationalen Fortbildung zugänglich ist, und die Technik ist das brauchbarste Schema dieser Art, das heute vorzufinden ist. Es gibt kein anderes, das mit ihr in Wettbewerb treten könnte, denn selbst die soziale Utopie verliert ihren Glanz, wenn sie sich nicht auf den technologischen Fortschritt stützt. Sie kann nicht auf ihn verzichten, ohne unglaubwürdig zu werden"[2].

Jünger hatte diese Positionsbestimmung nicht so unkritisch verstanden, wie sie hier auftritt – sondern die Begrenzungen benannt: „Wer auf die Technik Hoffnungen setzt – und die Hoffnung schließt eine Vorwegnahme des Zukünftigen in sich –, der muß sich darüber klar werden, daß er von der Technik das erwarten darf, was innerhalb ihrer Möglichkeiten liegt, und nichts anderes. Er muß von ihr absondern, was sich chimärisch an sie heftet und mit ihren Zwecken und Zielen nichts zu schaffen hat. Tut er das nicht, dann reist er mit Maschinen in die Mythologie, die der Verstand konstruiert hat" (ebd.).

Diese Überlegungen sind zu einem Zeitpunkt geschrieben, in dem das Revier eine technische Expansion in einer Größenordnung erlebte, die nur der der Nachkriegszeit der fünfziger bis siebziger Jahre entsprach. Die erste Phase im Übergang von 19. zum 20. Jahrhundert war kulturell gravierender, als sie die Wahrnehmungsgewohnheiten nachhaltig veränderte – die Ergebnisse der Technik wurden zur „Zweiten Natur". Das System begründete das, was heute rückblickend als Technische Kontradiktion bezeichnet werden kann: Kennzeichen eines gesellschaftlichen Wandels, bei dem der technische Sektor seit dem 19. Jahrhundert noch auf der behaupteten ‚Fortschrittlichkeit' der Entwicklung beharrte, während die eintreffenden empirischen Daten über die Krisenstandorte der Stadtentwicklung und

door, stays out of sight for a while, and then finally penetrates "through all our senses" into the "inmost parts of the soul" (Henning Ritter).

Jünger was describing the two-faced nature of technology when on the one hand he stated: "Utopia needs a system which is accessible to rational further education, and technology is the most useful system of this kind which can be found today. There is no other system capable of competing with it, because even social Utopia will lose its shine if it is not supported by technological progress. It cannot do without it, for fear of losing its credibility."[2]

Jünger did not regard this determination of position in the uncritical way in which it appears here, but stated its limitations. "Anyone who places his hopes in technology – and hope subsumes in itself anticipation of the future – must be quite clear in his own mind that he is allowed to expect something from technology which lies within the realms of its possibilities, and nothing more. He must separate everything from it that clings to it chimeristically and has nothing to do with its aims and purposes. If he does not do so, he will travel with machinery into the mythology which the mind has construed." (op. cit.)

These considerations were written down at a time in which the Ruhr was undergoing technical expansion of an order of magnitude only matched by the post-war decades from the 1950s to the 1970s. The first phase, the transition from the 19th to the 20th century, was culturally more drastic in the sense that it changed perceptive habits permanently. The results of technology became a "second Nature". The system laid the foundations that now, in retrospect, can be described as technical contradiction: the signs of social total change in which the technical sector has been insisting ever since the 19th century on the "progressive-

Zeche Nordstern in Gelsenkirchen, denkmalwerter Bau des Architekten Fritz Schupp/ Nordstern colliery in Gelsenkirchen, historically valuable construction by the architect Fritz Schupp

Bundesgartenschau 1997 auf dem Gelände der Zeche Nordstern/ Federal Garden Show 1997, site of the Nordstern colliery

Landschaftsarchitekten/landscape architects: Pridik & Partner, Marl
Fotos: Reinhart Wustlich

**Hallenskelett und Turm der Zeche Nordstern; Umbau der ehemaligen Lohnhalle in ein Bürogebäude/
Skeleton of the hall and tower of the Nordstern colliery; conversion of the former pay office hall into an office block**

Architekt/architect: Wolfgang Felder, Baucoop, Köln

die jahrelang betriebenen Reparatur- und Reaktivierungsanstrengungen bereits verdeutlichten, daß die nachfolgende Modernisierung von Standort und Wirtschaftsstruktur heute in erster Linie eine aufwendige Beseitigung, eine Kompensation von Technikfolgen bedeutet, die der Allgemeinheit hohe Kosten verursacht. Es kommt nicht von ungefähr, daß der Strukturwandel des Ruhrgebiets gerade dies, auch für andere Regionen, zu Bewußtsein bringt.

Aktivierte Landschaft – räumliche Lagerung In Gelsenkirchen grenzt an die Stadtteile Horst und Hessler eines der postindustriellen Projekte neuen Zuschnitts, das im Vergleich zum Landschaftspark Duisburg-Nord einen Schritt weitergeht. Auf dem 50 ha großen Gelände der Zeche Nordstern, dessen ökologische und ästhetische Aufwertung Thema der Bundesgartenschau 1997 sein wird (Landschaftsarchitekten: Pridik & Partner), erfolgt zwischen den Halden Eickwinkel und Schurenbach die Entwicklung unter konzeptionell ‚umgekehrten' Vorzeichen: „Am Anfang steht der landschaftsplanerische Entwurf, auf dessen Grundlage die Landschaft vorausgebaut wird. Der Städtebau und die Architektur einzelner Objekte haben sich dann einzupassen; sie folgen nach" (Karl Ganser). Mit der Umkehrung der Prozeßabfolge soll der Landschaftsverbrauch unterbunden werden. Das Konzept sieht vor, die Künstlichkeit der Industrielandschaft bei der Gestaltung des Landschaftsparks zu verstärken, die Zechengebäude des Architekten Fritz Schupp als Denkmale zu erhalten und Erweiterungsflächen für den Neubau von Gewerbe und Wohnen einzupassen. Die ehemalige Lohnhalle der Zeche und die anschließende Doppelhalle werden von Wolfgang Felder, Baucoop, zu Bürogebäuden umgebaut. Verlängerung der Nutzungsdauer bestehender Ge-

ness" of development, whilst the empirical data being received on the crisis-wracked locations of urban development and repair and reactivation efforts being pursued for years were already making it clear that the subsequent modernisation of location and business structure now signifies principally an expensive removal of and compensation for technological consequences which is involving the general public in heavy expense. There is good reason for the fact that the structural change in the Ruhr is bringing exactly this into people's consciousness, and in other regions as well.

Activated landscape – spatial storage
In Gelsenkirchen, bordering on the suburbs of Horst and Hessler, there is one of the postindustrial projects of a new kind, one that goes a step further in comparison with the Duisburg-Nord landscape park. The Nordstern colliery site covers 50 hectares (125 acres) and its ecological and aesthetic improvement will be the focus of the National Garden Show in 1997 (landscape architects: Pridik & Partners). Located between the Eickwinkel and the Schurenbach dumps, it is developing conceptionally "in the opposite direction", because: "It starts off from the landscape gardener's plan on the basis of which the landscape has to be prepared. Urban development and architecture follow then have to adapt to it; they follow along afterwards." This strengthens the position of the landscape park, retains the mine buildings of the architect Fritz Schupp as an ancient monument, and fits in additional areas for commercial and residential purposes. The former wages office of the mine and the double building alongside it are being converted into offices by Wolfgang Felder, of Baucoop. Lengthening the useful life of existing buildings means, in this case: reduction of old interiors, supplementing them with

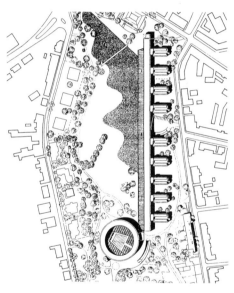

bäude heißt hier: Reduktion alter Einbauten, Ergänzung durch entwickelte Technik in elementierten, leichten Einheiten.

Die Umkehrung der Begründung von Gebäude- und Landschaftswerten, die Vermeidung von Landschaft als „ungestaltetem Rest" verweist auf einen Wandel der Wahrnehmung – die technologische Entwicklung hat ihren Raumanspruch zurückzunehmen. Sie hat neben einer offensiven Bewertung der ästhetischen Dimension des Landschaftsbildes bescheidener zu sein. Die Beziehung zwischen Architektur und Landschaft, die auf diese Weise anders balanciert wird, verschafft den Menschen emotionale Ausdehnung und Offenheit. Vielleicht läßt sich eine Ahnung von Kultiviertheit zurückgewinnen, die das Verhältnis von Stadt und Land vor der industriellen Revolution geprägt hat.

Gläserner Rand in der Stadt Bis zum Stadtkern Gelsenkirchens, fast bis an den

developed technology in light, elementised units.

The reversal of the basis for architectural and landscape values, and the avoidance of the landscape as an "undesigned residue", reveals a change in perception; technological development is required to relinquish its claim to livingspace, and to be more modest in the face of aggressive assessment of the aesthetic dimension of the landscape. The relationship between architecture and landscape, which in this way finds a different balance, provides people with emotional expansion and openness. Perhaps it is possible to regain a certain feeling of cultivation such as dominated the relationship between town and country before the industrial revolution.

The glass edge of the city Until 1988 a technically deformed bulge of landscape ran all the way to the centre of Gelsenkirchen, almost up to the mainline railway station. The heavy

Luftbild des Wissenschaftsparks Rheinelbe auf dem Gelände des ehemaligen Gußstahlwerks in Gelsenkirchen/
Aerial view of the Science park Rheinelbe on the site of the former cast steel plant
Foto: IBA Emscher Park

Wissenschaftspark Rheinelbe/Science park Rheinelbe
Architekten/architects: Uwe Kiessler + Partner, Munich
Fotos: Lukas Roth (1)

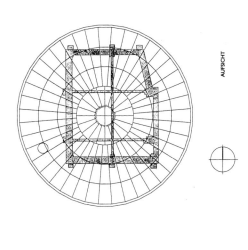

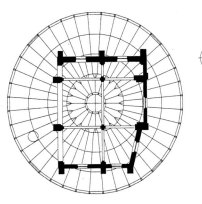

Evangelische Marktkirche in Essen, Konzept/ Protestant Marketchurch, Essen, conception

**Architekt/architect: Frank Ahlbrecht, Essen –
Tragwerksplanung/structural engineer:
Stefan Polònyi, Köln**

Hauptbahnhof, verlief bis 1988 noch eine technisch überformte Landschaftsbucht. Die Schwerindustrie des 19. Jahrhunderts hatte sich mit einem rauchenden Gußstahlwerk und mattverglasten Produktionshallen in die Stadt gefräst – ein Zusammenprall von unklarem städtischem Raum und raumbeanspruchender Technik. Das Projekt des Wissenschaftsparks Rheinelbe (Architekten: Uwe Kiessler & Partner; Landschaftsarchitekt: Peter Drecker) rekultiviert hier beschädigte Stadtlandschaft, die kaum stärker unter Spannung stehen konnte. Das Projekt entwickelt einerseits eine neue, gläserne Stadtkante. Es gibt andererseits dem überformten Naturraum in der Stadt etwas wieder zurück: einen Park mit Wasserflächen, eine neue Landschaft, die ein Stück weit aus den Zwängen der technischen Zivilisation entlassen wird. Es ist eine Erinnerung an Naturnähe, ein Rand inmitten des Festkörpers Stadt, der den Menschen erlaubt, sich auszudehnen: in die Szenerie einer Garten-Landschaft der Arbeit. Die große Gerade der Baustruktur des Wissenschaftszentrums legt eine dreihundert Meter lange Glasarkade an den neugewonnenen Park. Eine weiße Baustruktur mit Decks, Treppen und Galerien schließt sich an. Die angedockten Büropavillons der Forschungsinstitute (neue Techniken der Solarenergie und der Energie-Speicherung) bilden den offenen Kamm des Gebäudes nach Osten, zur alten Stadt. Hier findet die Erprobung einer neuen, leistungsfähigen Stadtstruktur Raum, ein Solarkraftwerk auf den Dächern eingeschlossen – eine technische Arkade des 21. Jahrhunderts.

Verlust immateriellen Reichtums Der Natur überformte Landschaft zurückgeben: Das Nachdenken über die Balance von Technik und Natur, von Landschaft und Stadt begann frühzeitig. Vergleichbare Positionen finden sich be-

industry of the 19th century had milled its way into the city with a smoking iron foundry and dull glazed production buildings, a collision between ill-defined urban space and the space-consuming demands of technology. The Rheinelbe Science Park project (architects: Uwe Kiesler & Partners; landscape architect: Peter Drecker) is recultivating the damaged urban landscape here, which could hardly be under greater tension. The project is on the one hand developing a new, glass edge for the city, on the other hand creating a park with lakes, a new landscape which will be released some way from the restrictions of technical civilisation. It is a reminder of the proximity of Nature, an edge in the middle of the solid city centre which will give human beings an opportunity to expand in a scenario of a garden-landscape of work. The long, straight section of the Science Centre's structure will consist of a glass arcade, 300 metres long, beside the newly regained park. A white building with decks, staircase, and galleries adjoins it. The office pavilions of the research institutes docking on to it (new techniques in solar energy and energy storage) form the open comb of the building to the east, towards the old city.

Here a new, efficient structure for space is being tried out, a solar power station included on the roof – a technical arcade of the 21st century.

Loss of intangible wealth Thinking about the balance between technology and Nature, about the landscape and the city, started at an early stage. Comparable positions can be found even with Friedrich Georg Jünger; he said, in "The Perfection of Technology", that the industrial landscape had lost its fertility and had become the location for mechanical production, and that this created a profound difference.

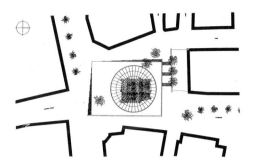

reits bei Friedrich Georg Jünger – die Industrielandschaft habe ihre Fruchtbarkeit verloren, heißt es in „Perfektion der Technik", sie sei Sitz mechanischer Produktion geworden, das schaffe einen tiefen Unterschied.

Die verlorene Landschaftsempfindung der Romantik wird nachvollziehbar: „Der Anblick eines Weinbergs, eines Obsthains, einer blühenden Landschaft erheitert, nicht wegen des Nutzens, den sie abwerfen, sondern weil eine Empfindung der Fruchtbarkeit, des Überflusses, des zwecklosen Reichtums in uns hervorgerufen wird ... Es ist zunächst ein Gefühl des Hungers, der uns in (der Industrielandschaft) beschleicht, vor allem in den Industriestädten und Industrielandschaften, in denen nach der metaphorischen Sprache des technischen Fortschritts eine „blühende" Industrie zu Hause ist ... Er ist so offenbar, daß selbst der Eindruck konzentrierter Macht, den wir in den Zentren der Schwerindustrie empfangen, ihn nicht überwindet"[3].

Die Idee nachhaltigen Wirtschaftens wurde auch in den dreißiger Jahren im Ansatz, vergeblich, formuliert: „Zu den Kennzeichen jeder geordneten Wirtschaft gehört, daß die bewirtschaftete Substanz erhalten und geschont wird, daß aller Verzehr vor jener Grenze haltmacht, deren Überschreiten diese Substanz selbst gefährdet oder vernichtet" (ebd.). Und: „Nicht nur die Bodenschätze, auch der Mensch gehört zu den Beständen, welche dem technischen Verzehr unterworfen werden".

Das post-fortschrittliche Stadium wird gleichermaßen im voraus beschrieben, der „Verbrauch der Technik" erstrecke sich auch auf die eigene Apparatur: „Die fortschreitende Technik füllt die Erde nicht nur mit ihren Maschinen und Werken, sie füllt sie auch mit dem technischen Gerümpel und Abfall. Dieses rostende Blech und Gestänge, diese zerbroche-

The lost feeling for the landscape that had existed in the Romantic Age becomes easier to understand: "A view of a vineyard, an orchard, a flowering landscape cheers the spirit, not because of their usefulness but because a feeling for their fertility, their productivity, their abundant wealth is evoked in us ... It is first of all a feeling of hunger that creeps over us (in the industrial landscape), particularly in the industrial cities and industrial landscapes in which, to use the metaphorical language of technical progress, a "flourishing" industry has its home ... It is so obvious that even the impression of concentrated power which we perceive in the centres of heavy industry cannot overwhelm it."[3]

The idea of perpetual business also started to be formulated, without success, in the 1930s: "It is one of the distinguishing features of any orderly economy that the assets being processed retain their value and are spared destruction, that any consumption must stop at the point at which any further consumption would itself endanger or destroy them" (op. cit.). And: "Not only mineral wealth but human kind itself is one of the assets which are subject to technical consumption."

The post-progressive stage is likewise described in advance, the "consumption of technology" extends to include one's own apparatus: "The progress of technology fills the world not only with machines and works but also with technological scrap and rubbish. This rusting steel plate or collection of pipes, these broken and useless machine parts, remind the thoughtful on-looker of the lack of durability, the ephemeral nature of the process to which they bear witness." In other words: "Wear and tear are also a form of consumption".

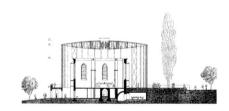

Verglaster Zylinder und aufgesetzte verglaste Kuppel als Einheit/ Glazed cylinder with a glass dome on top as a light unit: computer-aided calculation gives a filigree appearance

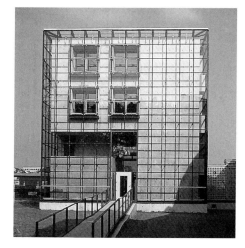

Galerie Architektur und Arbeit auf dem Gelände der stillgelegten Zeche Oberschuir in Gelsenkirchen/
The Gelsenkirchen Gallery of Architecture and Work on the worked-out site of the Oberschuir mine

Architekten/architects: Herbert Pfeiffer, Christoph Ellermann & Partner, Lüdinghausen
Fotos: Reinhart Wustlich

nen und verbeulten Maschinenteile erinnern den nachdenklichen Betrachter an die Vergänglichkeit und Flüchtigkeit des Vorgangs, dessen Zeuge er ist". Mit anderen Worten: „der Verschleiß ist eine der Formen des Konsums".

Technik der konstruktiven Sachlichkeit Technik heute weder als Chimäre noch als Mythologie zu verstehen, sondern als Aufgabe „konstruktiver Sachlichkeit", ist die Position, die Stefan Polònyi vertritt. Die Welt nicht den Massen des Vergänglichen auszuliefern, sondern Räume der Leichtigkeit und der Konzentration zu entwickeln, ist auch eine Frage konstruktiver Philosophie. Für eine veränderte Stufe des Technikverständnisses im Revier steht das Projekt der Marktkirche in Essen (Architekt: Frank Ahlbrecht). Ein Torso historischer Bausubstanz, die alte Marktkirche – von baulichen Verunstaltungen und Überformungen befreit. Eine neue gläserne, zylindrische Hülle soll den historischen Kern schützend umgreifen, zugleich aber eine eigene, freie Gestalt begründen. Die Idee der Glaskuppel und der Entwurf eines filigranen Tragwerks dafür werden als Beiträge einer „strukturellen Architektur" verstanden, welche die zeitgenössischen technischen Möglichkeiten nutzt, sie von herkömmlichen Konstruktionen absetzt und auf dekorative Wirkungen der Konstruktion verzichtet. Das Konzept der neuen Glas-Stahl-Konstruktion wird als freistehend und unabhängig von der vorhandenen Bausubstanz gedacht: verglaster Zylinder und aufgesetzte verglaste Kuppel bilden eine leichte Einheit. Computergestützte Rechenprozesse ermöglichen eine filigrane Erscheinung, die der Vorstellung von Entmaterialisierung nahekommt. Das Konzept der Seilkuppel auf Rohrstützen prägt die Konstruktion. Die technische Idee ähnelt dem Prinzip der leichten Speichenräder, das bis auf das 19.

The technology of constructive factualness Defining technology today neither as a chimera nor as mythology, but as the responsibility of "constructive factualness", is the position taken up by Stefan Polònyi. Developing spaces of lightness and concentration instead of exposing the world to the masses of ephemeral things is also a question of constructive philosophy. One project that symbolises a change in technological understanding is the Market Church in Essen (architect: Frank Ahlbrecht). The rump of a historical structure, the old Market Church has been liberated from deformity and deformation. A new, cylindrical glass shell is intended to surround and protect the historic core, and at the same time to form the basis of an individual, free figure. The idea of the glass dome and the design of a filigree supporting structure for it are defined as contributions to a "structural architecture" which makes use of modern technical possibilities, divorced from traditional constructions and dispensing with the decorative effects of the construction. The concept for the new glass and steel structure has been conceived as a free-standing design, independent of the existing building; a glazed cylinder with a glass dome on top form a light unit. Computer-aided calculation processes make it possible to give the whole a filigree appearance which brings it close to the idea of immaterialism. The concept of a cable dome on top of tubular supports dominates the design. The technical idea is similar to the principle of the light spoked wheel, which dates back to the 19th century. The figure on the dome is achieved by pre-tension, and spokes of various different lengths form the vaulting. At the top of the roof skin there is a lantern on the inner ring of the cable groups. The process of designing the structure is regarded as a process of searching with the

Jahrhundert zurückgeht. Die Figur der Kuppel wird durch eine Vorspannung erreicht, Spreizen unterschiedlicher Länge formen die Wölbung. Im Scheitel der Dachhaut entsteht auf dem inneren Ring der Seilverbände eine Laterne. Der Entwurfsvorgang wird als Suchprozeß verstanden, welcher auf die Minimierung der Konstruktion, auf die Vermeidung von Überflüssigem und auf den sparsamsten Materialverbrauch zielt. Technische Filigranität wird als Ausdruck „konstruktiver Sachlichkeit" verstanden.

Korrespondenz von Masse und Transparenz Bei der Anlage der Gelsenkirchener Galerie Architektur und Arbeit (Architekten: Herbert Pfeiffer, Christoph Ellermann und Partner) wird ein historisches Gebäude der stillgelegten Zeche Oberschuir aus dem Jahre 1909 zu einem strukturalistischen Neubau in Beziehung gesetzt. Alle hoch installierten Räume der Galerie werden in dem Neubau untergebracht. Zwischen dem erhaltenen Förderturm und dem Zechengebäude wurde ein skulpturaler Betonkubus errichtet, zu dessen klar geschnittenen Flächen die Auskantungen der Fenstergewände und die Einkerbungen der Gebäudegliederungen plastisch in Beziehung gesetzt wurden. Der gesamte Würfel wird von einer strukturellen Glashaut umhüllt, die auch die Dachanschlüsse übergreift. Die klare Hülle spielt die Wirkungen der Transparenz aus, der Betonkubus setzt die Qualitäten der Masse dagegen. Die Räume zwischen beiden Geometrien werden als diatherme Schichten, als Klimahülle, aufgefaßt. Raster und Fläche, Durchsichtigkeit und Geschlossenheit wirken zusammen. Je nach Perspektive und Belichtung wechseln Transparenz und Reflexion im Eindruck ab. Die minimierte Außenhaut, Zeichen avancierter Technologien, und die

aim of minimising the construction, avoiding anything superfluous, and making the most economical possible use of material. Technical filigree work is defined as the expression of "constructive factualness".

Correspondence of mass and transparency The Gelsenkirchen "Gallery of Architecture and Work" (architects: Herbert Pfeiffer, Christoph Ellermann & Partners) is setting a historic building on a worked-out mine site, Oberschuir, dating from 1909, into the context of a new structuralistic building. All the highly installed rooms in the gallery are accommodated in the new building. A sculptural concrete cube has been erected between the winding tower, which has been preserved, and the mine building, to the clear-cut surfaces of which the outer edges of the window walls and the notches of the building elements have been placed plastically in context. The whole cube is surrounded by a structural glass skin which also reaches across to connect with the roof. The clear shell plays out the effects of transparency, and the concrete cube sets up the qualities of mass against it. The spaces between both geometries are used as diathermal layers, forming a climate shell. Grids and areas, transparency and enclosure all interact with one another. Transparency and reflection make alternating impressions according to the point of view and the lighting. The minimised outside skin, a symbol of advanced technologies, and the modern concrete structure are counter-balanced by the massiveness of the traditional masonry of the mine. The old building accommodates the actual exhibition areas in the lovingly restored machinery hall. The two buildings are linked by a bridge, the surrounding areas of which are formed of glass bricks.

The vicinity of the traditional steel structures

Die Räume zwischen den Geometrien des Gebäudes: diatherme Schichten, Klimahülle/ The spaces between both geometries: diathermal layers, forming a climate shell

Technik und Produktionsstruktur/ Technology and production structure

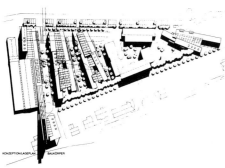

**Zukunftszentrum und Technologiepark in Herten – die aufgefächerte Struktur wird in den Bestand der Gebäude am Rand des Zentrums gelegt/
Futures centre and technology park in Herten – the building ensemble fans out amidst the existing buildings**

**Architekten/architects: Rüdiger Kramm und Axel Strigl, Darmstadt
Fotos: Lukas Roth (3)**

moderne Betonstruktur stehen der Massivität des traditionellen Mauerwerksbaus der Zeche gegenüber. Der Altbau nimmt die eigentlichen Ausstellungsflächen in der sorgfältig restaurierten Maschinenhalle auf. Beide Gebäude sind durch den Brückensteg verbunden, dessen Umfassungsflächen aus Glassteinen gebildet werden.

Die Nachbarschaft von traditionellem Stahlbau von Förderturm und Maschinenhalle, von historischem Mauerwerksbau des Zechengebäudes und filigraner Glashülle des Neubaus ist eine symbolische: auch sie beschreibt den Wandel von den schweren zu den leichten Technologien.

Technik und Produktionsstruktur Der Strukturwandel des Reviers zeigt genau dies: den Zwang zur Revision der Prinzipien von Technologie und Arbeit im Revier. Er schließt die Abwendung von den hermetischen Großstrukturen der alten Arbeitswelt ein: von den Kohleburgen der Zechen, den Katarakten der Kokereien mit ihren Gewitterwolken aus Dampf, von den Türmen der Hochofenbastionen, den Gußstahlhallen, den riesigen Walzstraßen, die in der Nachkriegszeit Garanten vieler und scheinbar sicherer Arbeitsplätze waren. Es waren zugleich Bastionen, die sich für eine ausgeglichene Entwicklung der Siedlungsstruktur als unverträglich erwiesen. Der Wandel der Technik aus dem System heraus und die globale Konkurrenz haben diese Bastionen ‚sicherer Arbeit' seit Jahrzehnten schleichend entwertet. Der Stahlarbeiter des sekundären Sektors wird im Extremfall zum dienstleistenden Reiseführer in den stillgelegten Stahlwerken und Zechen der neuen Landschaftsparks des Reviers. So tritt der „Konsum der Arbeitsplatzstrukturen" als letzter Faktor der Kette auf. Die neue Entwicklung ist durch einen Maßstabsbruch der indu-

of the winding tower and the machinery hall, of the historical brick masonry of the mine building and the filigree glass shell of the new building, is a symbolic one: this too describes the change from the heavy to the light technologies.

Technology and production structure
The structural change of the Ruhr shows exactly this: the compulsion to review the principles of technology and work in the Ruhr. It includes the rejection of the huge, hermetic structures of the old world of work, from the mountainous coal tips, the cataracts of the coking works with their storm-clouds of steam, from the towers of the furnace bastions, the iron-foundry buildings, the gigantic steel-rolling mills which in the post-war years were the guarantors of many apparently secure jobs. They were bastions at the same time which proved incompatible with a balanced development of settlement structure. The technological change from within the system and global competition have robbed these bastions of "secure jobs" surreptitiously of the value over a period of decades. The steelworker in the secondary sector has become, to take an extreme case, a tour guide showing tourists around the old steel works and mines in the new Ruhr landscape park. Thus the "consumption of the job structure" takes its place as the last factor in the chain. The new development is dominated by the termination of the criteria of the industrial structures and, with them, a change in the criteria of urban structures. It is perfectly possible that somebody who remembers the image of the old industries as "heroic" would not be able to take the particulate nature of the new trade completely seriously.

The conversion of the Ruhr from its basis in mining and steel, from the "heavy" technolo-

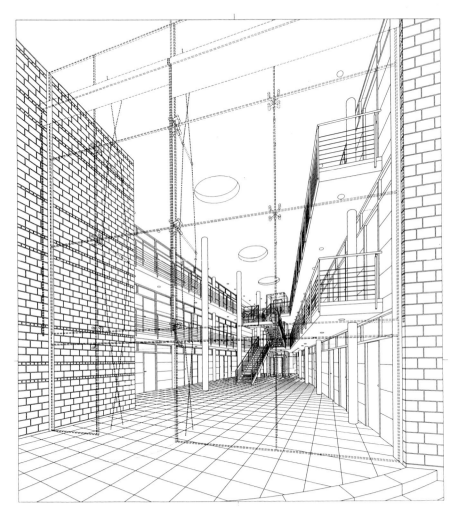

**Perspektivische Ansicht der Eingangshalle des Zukunftszentrums, Innenansicht aus dem Versammlungs- und Tagungsbereich/ Perspective drawing of the entrance hall of the Futures centre, interior view of the meeting and conference area
Foto: Kramm + Strigl**

striellen Strukturen und mit ihnen durch einen Maßstabswandel der Stadtstrukturen geprägt. Es ist leicht möglich, daß jemand, der das Bild der alten Industrien als ‚heroisch' in Erinnerung hat, die Kleinteiligkeit des neuen Gewerbes nicht so recht ernstzunehmen vermag. Die Umwandlung des Ruhrgebiets von einer Basis des Bergbaus und des Stahls, von einer Basis der ‚schweren' Technologien des 19. und frühen 20. Jahrhunderts zu einer den Menschen zugegies of the 19th and early 20th century, to one of a megalopolis orientated towards people, to a network of locations of the "light" technology of the 21st century, has already been initiated. The new forms of diversity and particulate work, however, which are intended to secure the future have still to prove their worth.

Transparency in the heart of the city
Reaching into the structure of the city centre of

Die Korrespondenz zwischen Alt und Neu zum künstlerischen Kontrast erhoben – das Schwarz betont das traditionelle Siedlungshaus. Die Situation der Erneuerung: Kopfbau des Zukunftszentrums mit Eingangshalle und Glashaus als Dachabschluß. Die Schräge vor der Front wird aus Solarkollektoren gebildet/
The relationship between old and new raised to the status of an artistic contrast – black emphasizes the traditional worker's estate house. Completed reconstruction: the front building of the Futures centre with entrance hall and roof-top glass house. The slanted façade element consists of solar collectors

wandten Megalopole, zu einem Netz von Standorten ‚leichter' Technologien des 21. Jahrhunderts, ist eingeleitet. Die neuen Formen der Vielfalt und der Kleinteiligkeit der Arbeit, die Zukunft sichern sollen, haben sich allerdings noch zu beweisen.

Transparenz am Stadtkern In die Struktur des Hertener Stadtkerns eingreifend, hat die Entwicklung des Zukunfts- und Technologiezentrums begonnen (Architekten: Rüdiger Kramm und Axel Strigl), Alternativen für die Arbeit zu entwickeln. Am Standort einer ehemaligen Maschinenfabrik – und dessen aufgelassene Montagehalle nutzend, entstand ein Büro- und Laborgebäude als Kopfbau einer städtebaulichen Achse, welche die Verbindung zur Innenstadt begründen soll. Die auf die Fuge nahe Kombination alter Baustrukturen und transparenter Glasarchitektur verdeutlicht den

Herten, the development of the Future and Technology Centre (architects: Rüdiger Kramm and Axel Strigl) has already begun to develop alternatives to work. On the site of a former engineering factory, and making use of its deserted work shop hall, an office and laboratory building has been created as the head end of an urban axis which is intended to form the link to the inner city centre. The combination close to the join between old building structures and transparent glass architecture demonstrates the change of conditions to the light technologies of what is now the next generation but one in technical development: research into the micro-biology of environmental protection, later the salvaging of raw materials and waste-disposal technology.

The basic idea consists of changing the commercial or industrial use, which used to disturb the neighbourhood, in a compatible way in

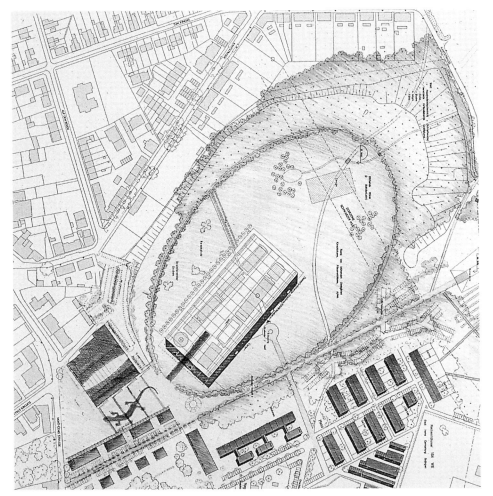

Lageplan: Führungsakademie des Innenministers Nordrhein-Westfalen in Herne-Sodingen; der große Hallenraum des Glashauses inmitten des umgebenden Parks – viergeschossige Glashülle als technische Folie, die Innen- und Außenwelt voneinander trennt/
Site plan: Academy of adult education in Herne-Sodingen; the large glasshouse hall in the surrounding park – the four-storey glass shell as a technical screen, separating inside from outside

Architekten/architects: Françoise-Hélène Jourda, Gilles Perraudin, Lyon; Manfred Hegger, Doris Hegger-Luhnen, Günter Schleiff, Kassel;
Landschaftsarchitekten/landscape architects: Peter Latz + Partner, Kranzberg; Michel Desvignes, Versailles

Wandel der Bedingungen zu den leichten Technologien der inzwischen übernächsten Generation technischer Entwicklung: Forschung der Mikrobiologie im Umweltschutz, später Wertstoffrückgewinnung und Entsorgungstechnologie.

Die Grundüberlegung besteht darin, die früher störende, für die Nachbarschaft belastende gewerbliche oder industrielle Nutzung verträglich zu wandeln, um mit der Erneuerung order at the same time to give a signal through the renewal of the programmes and the architecture for the change in the mixture of different uses in the urban area. The controlled change in production processes requires a deliberate gain in experience in order to be able to attain more compact and at the same time lighter structures in the city.

The head end of the Future Centre, dominated by the steel supporting work of the air-con-

Einlagerung des Glashauses in die Landschaft, Einbeziehung in die natürlichen Luftströmungen und Kühlung durch Wasserflächen/
Insertion of the glasshouse into the landscape, taking advantage of natural currents of air and of the cooling element of water
Fotos: Jourda + Perraudin

der Programme und der Architektur zugleich ein Signal für den Wandel der Mischung unterschiedlicher Nutzungen im Stadtbereich zu geben. Die kontrollierte Veränderung der Produktionsprozesse erfordert den gezielten Erfahrungsgewinn, um zu kompakteren, zugleich leichteren Strukturen in der Stadt zu kommen.

Der Kopfbau des Zukunftszentrums, durch ein Stahltragwerk mit Klimahülle geprägt, trägt

ditioned shell, carries a glass-house as a sloping end to the roof. The structure presents a symbol of dynamic forces for the new beginning in urban structural change. Its transparency at the same time forms a landmark in the historically determined structure of the urban surroundings.

Ecological technology as a large building A new generation of architecture inclu-

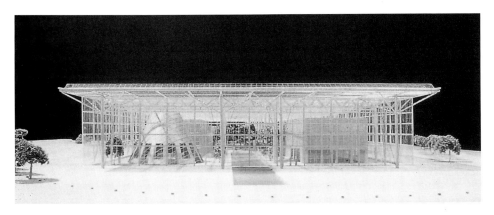

Modell des Hallenraumes mit Einbauten für die Funktionsbereiche im Inneren der Halle/ Model of the hall interior with inserted functional units in its centre
Foto: Jourda + Perraudin

ein Glashaus als auffallenden Dachabschluß. Der Bau vermittelt ein Zeichen von Dynamik für den Neubeginn des städtischen Strukturwandels. Seine Transparenz bildet zugleich ein Merkzeichen in der historisch bestimmten Struktur des städtebaulichen Umfeldes.

Ökologische Technologie als Hallenraum Zu einer neuen Generation von Architektur gehört das Konzept des großen Hallenraums unter Glas für die Führungsakademie des Innenministers Nordrhein-Westfalens in Herne-Sodingen (Architekten: Françoise-Hélène Jourda, Gilles Perraudin zusammen mit Manfred Hegger, Doris Hegger-Luhnen, Günter Schleiff; Landschaftsarchitekten: Peter Latz + Partner, Michel Desvignes). Über die filigrane Struktur einer avancierten Holzkonstruktion entwickelt sich eine viergeschossige Glashülle, die als technische Folie die Innen- von der Außenwelt der Akademie trennt. Die Gärten, Gebäudezeilen und Einbauten im Inneren profitieren (ähnlich dem Technologiezentrum in Moers) vom eigenen Schutz der Hülle, die nicht zuletzt im mitteleuropäischen Winter eine nahezu mediterrane Klimazone zu etablieren vermag.

des the concept of the large, internally open building under a glass roof for the Management Academy of the Minister of the Interior of North-Rhine / Westphalia in the Sodingen district of Herne (architects: Françoise-Hélène Jourda, Gilles Perraudin, together with Manfred Hegger, Doris Hegger-Luhnen, and Günter Schleiff; landscape architects: Peter Latz & Partners, Michel Desvignes). Under the filigree structure of an advanced wooden structure, a four-storey glass shell emerges which separates the inner world of the Academy from the outer world like a technical foil. The gardens, buildings, and interiors profit (like the Technology Centre in Moers) from the shelter of the shell, which is able to establish an almost Mediterranean climate zone even in the central European winter.

Anmerkungen: 1 Wandel ohne Wachstum, Stadt-Bau-Kultur im 21. Jahrhundert, Katalog zur VI. Architektur Biennale Vendig 1996, Kunibert Wachten (Hrsg.), S. 78 **2** Friedrich Georg Jünger, Die Perfektion der Technik, Frankfurt a.M. 1953/1980 **3** ebd.

Notes: 1 Wandel ohne Wachstum – Stadt-Bau-Kultur im 21. Jahrhundert (Change without growth – urban architectural culture: Catalogue of the VI. Architecture Biennale, 1996, Kunibert Wachten (ed.), page 78 **2** Friedrich Georg Jünger, Die Perfektion der Technik, Frankfurt am Main, 1953/1980 **3** op. cit.

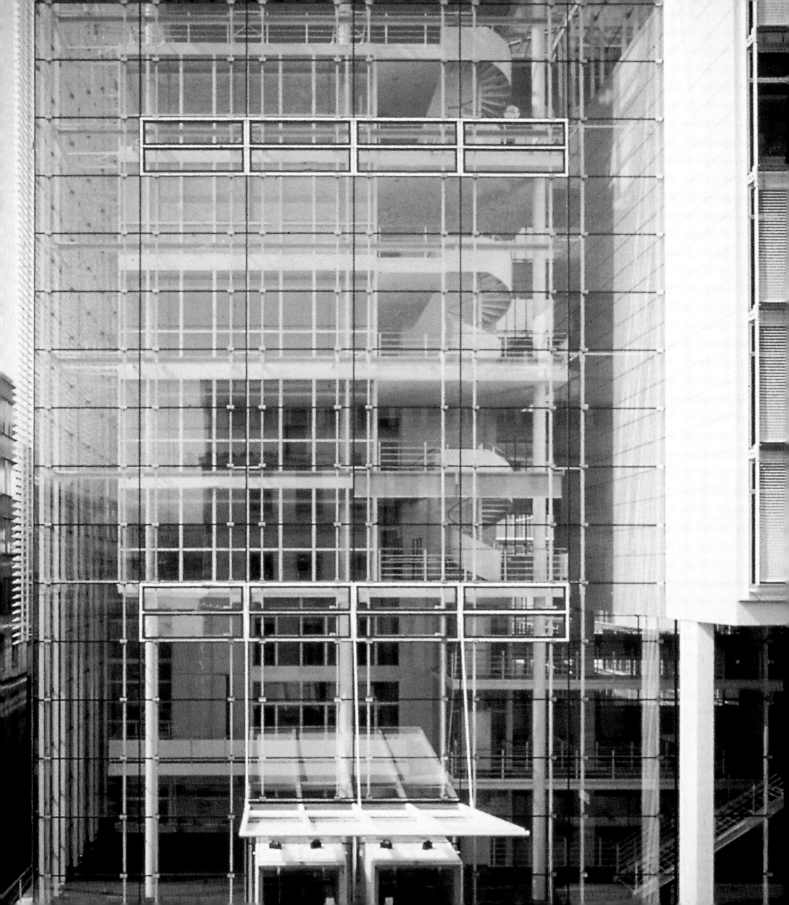

CONSTRUCTEC-PREIS 1996 — CONSTRUCTEC PRIZE 1996

Ziele Aus Anlaß der Internationalen Fachmesse für Technische Gebäudesysteme, Bautechnik und Architektur – CONSTRUCTEC '96, die vom 6. bis 9. November 1996 in Hannover stattfindet, wird der CONSTRUCTEC-PREIS zum fünften Mal verliehen.

Der Europäische Preis für Industriearchitektur wird von der Deutschen Messe AG, Hannover, gestiftet, in Zusammenarbeit mit dem Bund Deutscher Architekten BDA ausgelobt und als Anerkennung für hervorragende Leistungen auf dem Gebiet des Industriebaus vergeben.

Der Industriebau gab zu Beginn dieses Jahrhunderts der Architektur der damaligen Zeit wichtige Impulse. In den zwanziger und dreißiger Jahren entstanden Industriebauten, zum Beispiel von Walter Gropius, Peter Behrens, J. A. Brinkman und L. C. van der Vlugt, Williams und Trucco, die Vorbild für die moderne Architektur wurden. Mit dem Wandel von der Industrie- zur Informations- und Dienstleistungsgesellschaft sind die Anforderungen an die Gestaltung von Arbeitsstätten, besonders unter Aspekten wie Ressourcenschonung und Kosteneinsparung, weiter gewachsen. Vor allem aus diesen Gründen zählt die Architektur der künftigen Arbeitswelt zu den wichtigsten Herausforderungen der Gegenwart.

Die Deutsche Messe AG hat sich deshalb – erneut und gemeinsam mit dem Bund Deutscher Architekten BDA – zum Ziel gesetzt, mit dem CONSTRUCTEC-PREIS 1996 die Aufmerksamkeit auf gute und herausragende Beispiele aktueller Industriearchitektur zu lenken.

Themen und Teilnahmebereich Der Preis wird verliehen für ein nach 1992 in Europa errichtetes Bauwerk, das einer oder mehreren der folgenden Nutzungen dient:
- Produktion oder Lagerung von Waren,

Targets The CONSTRUCTEC PRIZE will be awarded for the fifth time on the occasion of the International Fair for Technical Building Systems, Building Technique and Architecture – CONSTRUCTEC '96, which will take place in Hanover from November 6th – 9th, 1996.

The European Prize for Industrial Architecture will be promoted by the Deutsche Messe AG, Hanover, organized in conjunction with the Bund Deutscher Architekten BDA, and awarded in recognition of excellent performances in the field of industrial construction.

In the beginning of this century, industrial construction was an important incentive to the architecture of those days. Throughout the twenties and thirties e.g. Walter Gropius, Peter Behrens, J. A. Brinkman and L. C. van der Vlugt, Williams and Trucco developed industrial buildings which became exemplary for modern architecture. With society changing from an industrial to an information and service era, demands for designing work places have continued to increase whereby particular emphasis is being placed on the saving of resources and costs. Hence, architecture of the future working world must be regarded as one of the most important challenges in these days.

Together with the Bund Deutscher Architekten BDA, the Deutsche Messe AG strives to again draw attention to good and excellent examples of present-day industrial architecture by awarding the CONSTRUCTEC PRIZE 1996.

Themes and Eligibility The Prize will be awarded by for a building completed in Europe after 1992, which serves one or several of the following purposes:
- production and storage of goods,
- production-directed research,
- exploiting natural resources and energy,

- produktionsorientierte Forschung,
- Rohstoff- und Energiegewinnung,
- Rückgewinnung und Wiederaufbereitung von Materialien,
- Abfallentsorgung.

Teilnahmeberechtigt sind Architektinnen und Architekten, die die geistigen Urheber der in Dokumentation eingereichten Bauwerke sind.

Beurteilung Entscheidend für die Vergabe des Preises und der Auszeichnungen ist der Gesamteindruck der Bauwerke, wie er der Jury durch die Bewerbungsunterlagen vermittelt wird.

Die Beurteilung folgt den Kriterien
- städtebauliche Einbindung,
- architektonische Qualität,
- ressourcenschonende Bauweisen,
- technische Innovationen,
- funktionale Aspekte,
- angemessene Innovations- und Folgekosten.

Preis und Auszeichnungen Der CONSTRUCTEC-PREIS ist mit DM 30.000,– dotiert und wird an den oder die geistigen Urheber des Bauwerks vergeben.

Bauherr, Architekten und andere maßgeblich beteiligte Planer erhalten jeweils eine Urkunde. Die Plakette „CONSTRUCTEC-PREIS 1996" sollte am Bauwerk befestigt werden.

Neben dem Preis erhalten Bauherr, Architekten und andere Planer von bis zu zehn weiteren Bauwerken besondere Auszeichnungen in Form von Urkunden.

Jury Die Mitglieder der international besetzten Jury:

IR. Mels Crouwel, Amsterdam (NL), Architekt

- recovering and reprocessing materials,
- waste management.

Eligible are architects who are the intellectual authors of the submissions.

Adjudication Criteria Decisive for awarding the prize and distinctions is the overall impression conveyed by the building resp. by the documents submitted to the Jury.

The Jury follows the criteria:
- urban insertion,
- architectural quality,
- resource-saving building procedures,
- technical innovations,
- functional aspects,
- appropriate investment and maintenance costs.

Prize and Distictions The CONSTRUCTEC PRIZE amounts to DM 30,000.– and will be handed over to the intellectual author(s) of the building.

The client, architects and all those responsibly involved in the planning procedure, will receive a certificate. The plaque "CONSTRUCTEC PRIZE 1996" should be fixed to the building.

Apart from this prize, special distinctions in form of certificates will be handed over to clients, architects and other planners up to 10 more buildings.

Jury Members of the internationally engaged Jury:

IR. Mels Crouwel, Amsterdam (NL), Architect

Prof. Dipl.-Ing. Klaus Daniels, Munich (D), Consulting Engineer, ETH Zurich

Dipl.-Ing. Dörte Gatermann, Cologne (D), Architect BDA

Dipl.-Arch. Jesper Gottlieb, Hellerup (DK), Architect M.A.A.

Sepp D. Heckmann, Hanover (D), Member of the Deutsche Messe AG Board

Dipl.-Ing. Andreas Gottlieb Hempel, Munich (D), President of the Bund Deutscher Architekten BDA

Prof. Dr.-Ing. Thomas Herzog, Munich (D), Architect BDA, Munich Technical University

Prof. Dipl.-Ing. Bernd Steigerwald, Potsdam (D), Architect and Consulting Engineer, FH Potsdam

Prof. Dipl.-Ing. Frank Werner, Münster (D), Architecture Historian, Wuppertal University – Comprehensive High-School

Preliminary Examination:
Dr.-Ing. Reinhart Wustlich, Hennef

Secretary to the Jury:
Dipl.- rer.pol. Carl Steckeweh, Bonn

Chairman of the Jury Meeting held in Hanover on June 19th, 1996, has been **Thomas Herzog**.

EMPA – Eidgenössische Materialprüf- und Forschungsanstalt/Material research centre, St. Gallen (CH) – Teilansicht/ detail view: Entwurf des CONSTRUCTEC-Preiträgers 1996/design of the CONSTRUCTEC Prize winner 1996:
Theo Hotz, Architekt/architect BSA, Zürich/ Zurich (CH)

Participants and Jury Decision   49 projects have been submitted from ten countries: Germany (17), Spain (8), Austria (4), Great Britain (3), Switzerland (10), Belgium (3),

EMPA – Eidgenössische Materialprüf- und Forschungsanstalt/Material research centre, St. Gallen (CH) – Teilansicht/Detail view
Fotos: Theo Hotz (3)

(10), Belgien (3), Frankreich (2), Niederlande (1), Tschechien (1), Japan (1). Die aus Japan eingereichte Arbeit ist in der Bundesrepublik Deutschland realisiert worden und damit teilnahmeberechtigt.

Nach Auffassung der Jury sind die meisten der eingereichten Arbeiten von hoher gestalterischer Qualität und – auch unter den Aspekten Investitions- und Folgekosten, Nutzungsqualität und -variabilität, Energieeinsparung und Verwendung moderner Gebäudetechnik – gute und repräsentative Beispiele für den gegenwärtigen Industriebau in Europa. Bei ihrer Entscheidung hat die Jury ausdrücklich den Mut zu qualitätvollen, aber auch unkonventionellen Lösungen anerkannt. Die ausgezeichneten Beispiele machen deutlich, daß hohe gestalterische und technische Qualität auch im Industriebau nicht vorrangig eine Frage von Kosten und Terminen ist, sondern dann erreicht wird, wenn alle Projektbeteiligten gut kooperieren und gemeinsam entwickelten Zielen folgen.

Mit dem **CONSTRUCTEC-PREIS 1996** wurden nach ausführlicher Debatte und einstimmiger Entscheidung drei Arbeiten gemeinsam ausgezeichnet, die vom gleichen Architekten stammen, d.h. im Sinne der Gesamtleistung seiner Person – jedoch jedem Bauwerk für sich gewidmet. Eine entsprechende Änderung des Auslobungstextes ist im vorhinein einstimmig verabschiedet worden.

CONSTRUCTEC-PREIS 1996: Theo Hotz, Zürich (CH), Architekt BSA, für die Gebäude
EMPA – Eidgenössische Materialprüf- und Forschungsanstalt, St. Gallen (CH),
ABB Kraftwerke AG Engineering, Forschung und Entwicklung, Baden (CH),
Betriebsgebäude Gaswerkareal – Städtische Werke Winterthur (CH).

France (2), the Netherlands (1), the Czech Republic (1), Japan (1).

The project submitted by Japan has been realized in Germany and is thus eligible.

In the Jury's opinion, most of the projects submitted reflect a high degree of creative quality, and are good and representative examples of today's industrial construction in Europe, even if considered under various other aspects, such as investment and maintenance costs, quality and variability of utilization, energy savings, and application of modern building technique. In making its decisions, the Jury expressively appreciated the courage of finding both solutions of high quality and of unconventional character. The distinguished examples reveal that high creative and technical quality of industrial construction are primarily not a question of costs and deadlines, but are being achieved by good co-operation and jointly developed objectives of all those participating in the project.

The **CONSTRUCTEC PRIZE 1996** has been awarded after detailed debates by unanimous decision jointly to three projects whose author is one and the same architect, but it is attributed to each single building. An appropriate alteration of the relevant text has previously been agreed upon by unanimity of votes.

The **CONSTRUCTEC PRIZE 1996: Theo Hotz,** Zurich (CH), Architect BSA, awarded to the buildings EMPA – Eidgenössische Materialprüf- und Forschungsanstalt, St. Gallen (CH),
ABB Kraftwerke AG Engineering, Forschung und Entwicklung, Baden (CH),
Betriebsgebäude Gaswerkareal – Städtische Werke Winterthur (CH).

Der Preis ist gleichermaßen den Architekten und den Ingenieuren, die das Bauwerk geplant haben, zugedacht.

Insgesamt acht **besondere Auszeichnungen** wurden folgenden Objekten zuerkannt:
M. Althammer + R. Hochuli, Zürich (CH), Architekten SIA, für die
- Uhrenfabrik Corum, La Chaux-de-Fonds (CH);

C. Baumschlager & D. Eberle, Lochau (A), Architekten, für das
- Gebäude Lager-Technik, Wolfurt (A);

CEPEZED/BV, Delft (NL), Architekten, für das
- Zentrum zur Erforschung humaner Arzneimittel, Leiden (NL);

Herzog & de Meuron, Basel (CH), Architekten, für das
- SBB-Stellwerk, Basel (CH);

Andreas Ortner, Graz (A), Architekt, für den
- Hallenneubau A. & C. Wallner, Scheifling (A);

Dominique Perrault, Paris (F), Architekt, für die
- Wasseraufbereitungsanlage Sagep, Paris (F);

Arturo Sanz, ACME, Valencia (E), Architekten, für das
- Inelcom-Werk, Valencia (E);

Schulitz + Partner, Braunschweig, Architekten BDA, für das
- Institut für Angewandte Mikroelektronik, Braunschweig (D).

The Prize is equally dedicated to the architects and the engineers who planned the buildings.

Eight **CONSTRUCTEC Awards** have been granted to the following projects:
M. Althammer + R. Hochuli, Zurich (CH), Architects SIA, to the
- Clock Manufacturing Plant Corum, La Chaux-de-Fonds (CH);

C. Baumschlager & D. Eberle, Lochau (A), Architects, to the
- Building Store-Technology, Wolfurt (A);

CEPEZED/BV, Delft (NL), Architects, to the
- Research Centre Human Pharmaceutics, Leiden (NL);

Herzog & de Meuron, Basel (CH), Architects, to the
- SBB Signal Box, Basel (CH);

Andreas Ortner, Graz (A), Architect, to the
- Workshop A. & C. Wallner, Scheifling (A);

Dominique Perrault, Paris (F), Architect, to the
- Water Purification Plant for Sagep, Paris (F);

Arturo Sanz, ACME, Valencia (E), Architects, to the
- Inelcom Plant, Valencia (E);

Schulitz und Partner, Braunschweig (D), Architects BDA, to the
- Institute of Micro-Electronics in Braunschweig (D).

CONSTRUCTEC-Preis 1996
Europäischer Preis für
Industriearchitektur

CONSTRUCTEC Prize 1996
European Prize for Industrial
Architecture

CONSTRUCTEC Prize 1996

Kommentar der Jury Der Architekt Theo Hotz hat drei Projekte eingereicht, die nach dem Urteil der Jury als architektonisch herausragend zu beurteilen sind.

Die außergewöhnliche Qualität der Bauten sowohl in städtebaulicher als auch in architektonischer und konstruktiver Hinsicht, sowohl nach Kriterien des Umgangs mit Energie als auch solchen der Nachhaltigkeit, führten zum einstimmig beschlossenen Votum der Jury, den drei Gebäuden gemeinsam den CONSTRUCTEC-Preis 1996 zuzuerkennen. Auf die Hervorhebung nur eines der Gebäude wurde verzichtet. Vielmehr wird zusätzlich zur Anerkennung der Leistung des Entwurfs und der Planung, der Ausführung und der offenkundig durchweg geglückten Kooperation mit den Bauherren als weitere besondere Qualität erkannt, mit welcher Klarheit und Disziplin bei den eingereichten Arbeiten in jedem Einzelfall die Grundrisse organisiert, Teile der Baukörper und die Gesamterscheinung überzeugend proportioniert und modernste Technologie souverän, ohne Anflug von modischen, kurzlebigen Attitüden eingesetzt und zu differenzierten Gesamtkonfigurationen integriert wurden.

Beschreibungen, Zeichnungen, Details und die fotografische Dokumentation sind gleichermaßen von hohem Niveau. Die Beschränkung auf sachliche Schwarz-Weiß-Darstellungen und der genaue Nachweis der technischen Einzelheiten speziell dort, wo dies die Tauglichkeit der z.T. sehr ambitionierten Systemlösungen der Fassaden angeht, präsentiert die Bauwerke unverstellt dem kritischen Urteil. Die ausgezeichneten Arbeiten zeigen auf diese Weise ihre herausragende architektonische Qualität als mustergültige, maßstabsetzende Industriebauten.

Comments by the Jury The architect Theo Hotz has submitted three projects whose architecture the Jury adjudicated as outstanding.

The exceptional quality of the buildings both from an urban point-of-view and with regard to their architecture and construction, complying with energy-saving and sustainability criteria, has led to the unanimous vote of the Jury to award the 1996 CONSTRUCTEC-Prize jointly to the three buildings. The idea of emphasizing the quality of one single building was dismissed. In addition to appreciating the performance of design and planning, execution and obviously successful cooperation with the clients, special recognition was attributed to the fact that ground-plans of each individual submission were outlined with utmost clearness and discipline, parts of the building body and total image convincingly proportioned, with complete command over most recent technology, but without taking recourse to modern shortlived attitudes, and integrated into differentiated configurations overall.

Of equal high quality are the descriptions, drawings, details and the photographic documentation. Restricting reproductions to objective black and white, and exact evidence of technical details, especially in instances where usefulness was required for partly very ambitious façade system solutions, presents the buildings to critical adjudication undisguised. Thus, the excellent works demonstrate their outstanding architectural quality as industrial buildings of exemplary standard.

Because of the importance of the theme and the technical solutions found, aspects of building climatics, energy economy and building technique were separately appreciated.

Preisträger/Laureate:
Theo Hotz, Architect BSA, Zürich, Zurich (CH)

Projekte/Projects:
EMPA – Eidgenössische Materialprüf- und Forschungsanstalt, St. Gallen (CH)
ABB Kraftwerke AG Engineering, Forschung und Entwicklung, Baden (CH)
Betriebsgebäude Gaswerkareal – Städtische Werke Winterthur (CH)

CONSTRUCTEC-Preis 1996

ABB Kraftwerke AG Engineering, Forschung und Entwicklung, Baden (CH)

ABB Kraftwerke AG Engineering, Forschung und Entwicklung/Engineering centre, Baden (CH)

Bauherren/clients:
Winterthur-Lebensversicherungsgesellschaft/Aargauische Beamtenpensionskasse/Pensionskasse der Schweizerischen Bankgesellschaft und Pensionskasse des Basler Staatspersonals
Architekt/architect:
Theo Hotz, Architekt BSA, Zürich/Zurich (CH)
Technische Gebäudeausrüstung/technical equipment:
Polke, Ziege, von Moos, Zürich/Zurich – Hefti, Hess, Martignoni, Aarau (CH)
Tragwerksplanung/structural engineering:
Minikus, Witta und Voss, Bauingenieure, Baden (CH)
Fertigstellung/date of completion: 1995
Fotos: Markus Fischer (6)

Wegen der Aktualität des Themas und der gefundenen baulich-technischen Lösungen wurden Aspekte der Bauklimatik, der Energiewirtschaft und der Gebäudetechnik einzeln gewürdigt.

Die Präzision der Konstruktion und des architektonischen Ausdrucks prägen das Gebäude der ABB Kraftwerke AG Engineering, Forschung und Entwicklung.

In der Struktur und in der Gestalt der Architektur soll sich die Identität des Gebäudes wie auch die Art ausdrücken, in der das Unternehmen denkt, arbeitet – und im Inneren des Gebäudes: lebt. Das innere Geschehen wird mit der Bauform visualisiert und den Mitarbeitern und Kunden fühlbar mitgeteilt.

Die Bauherren legten großen Wert darauf, daß die Spitzenqualität der in diesem Gebäude zukünftig zu erbringenden Engineeringleistungen einen ebenbürtigen architektonischen Ausdruck finden.

Die von den Mitarbeitern definierten Qualitäten – wie: Kommunikations- und Teamfähigkeit, Innovationsvermögen und Flexibilität –, finden in Struktur und Sprache der Architektur ihre Entsprechung.

Kommentar der Jury Der Baukörper des Forschungs- und Entwicklungsgebäudes der ABB zeigt in überzeugender Art den Umgang mit Bau- und Fassadenelementen zur Optimierung der Nutzung bei gleichzeitiger Minimierung des gebäudetechnischen Aufwandes und der Energiekosten. Durch differenzierte Fassadenausbildungen nach Nutzungsbereichen und Himmelsrichtungen sowie Nutzung von Speichermassen, ergänzt durch eine „intelligente" Gebäudetechnik, ergibt sich ein hervorragendes Zusammenwirken von Architektur, Konstruktion und Gebäudetechnik.

Precision of construction and architectural expression characterise the building housing the Research & Development section of ABB Kraftwerke AG Engineering, Baden (CH), designed by the Zurich architect Theo Hotz.

The structure and form of the architecture should reflect the identity and type of the building in which the company thinks, works and, within which, it lives. Internal events are expressed by the building design and are communicated clearly to the employees and customers.

The clients emphasised that the high quality of future engineering work to be carried out in the building should be reflected by an architectural expression of equal standing.

The qualities, as defined by the employees, i.e. the ability to communicate and work within a team, innovative ability and flexibility, are displayed in the structure and in the message communicated by the architecture.

Comments by the Jury The building body of the „Forschungs- und Entwicklungsgebäudes der ABB" convincingly demonstrates the application of construction and façade elements with a view to optimizing utilisation and simultaneously minimizing building technique installations and costs of energy. By forming façades differently to comply with utilization areas and sky directions, and by making use of storage places, enhanced by an „intelligent" building technique, an outstanding combination is obtained consisting of architecture, construction and building technique.

CONSTRUCTEC Prize 1996

ABB Kraftwerke AG, Engineeringgebäude:
Eingangshalle; Gebäudefuge/Engineering
centre: entrance hall; joint of buildings

CONSTRUCTEC-Preis 1996

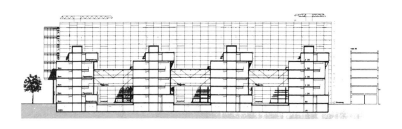

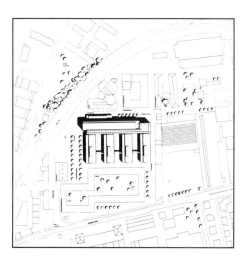

ABB Kraftwerke AG, Engineeringgebäude:
Lageplan; Grundrisse; Längsschnitt/
Engineering centre: site plan; floor plans;
longitudinal section

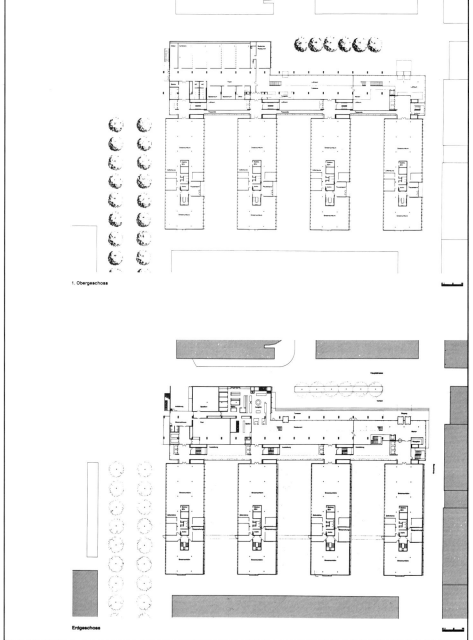

CONSTRUCTEC Prize 1996

**ABB Kraftwerke AG, Engineeringgebäude:
Eingangsgebäude; Casino/
Engineering centre: entrance building;
casino**

**Betriebsgebäude Gaswerkareal –
Städtische Werke Winterthur (CH)**

CONSTRUCTEC Prize 1996

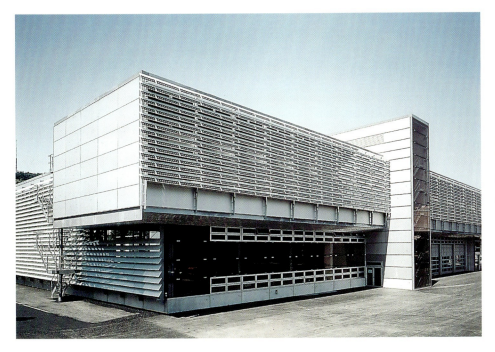

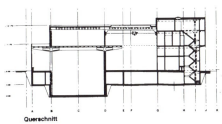
Querschnitt

Betriebsgebäude Gaswerkareal – Städtische Werke/Work shop centre, Winterthur (CH)

Bauherr/client:
Stadtverwaltung Winterthur, Departement Bau, Abt. Hochbauten, Winterthur (CH)
Architekt/architect:
Theo Hotz, Architekt BSA, Zürich/Zurich (CH)
Technische Gebäudeausrüstung/technical equipment:
Meier + Wirtz AG, Winterthur (CH)
Tragwerksplanung/structural engineering:
Ingenieurbüro Werner Höhn, Winterthur (CH)
Fertigstellung/date of completion: 1996
Fotos: Markus Fischer (8)

Vier sich durchdringende Volumen bilden das technische Ensemble des Betriebsgebäudes der Städtischen Werke, das der Zürcher Architekt Theo Hotz in Winterthur (CH) realisiert hat. Die auf die Volumen bezogene Konzeption ermöglicht eine abgestufte Reaktion auf das unterschiedlich ausgeprägte Umfeld der Stadt mit seiner je eigenen Maßstäblichkeit. Es tritt zur Zürcherstraße in seiner gesamten Dimension ablesbar als Industriebau in Erscheinung und stuft sich im rückwärtigen Teil auf die Höhe der zukünftig zu realisierenden Wohnbebauungen ab.

Die Gebäudeteile erfüllen unterschiedliche funktionale Anforderungen. Der Hauptbaukörper nimmt die Hauptwerkstatt und die Fahrzeughalle auf. Der Lagerteil ist aus klimatischen und betrieblichen Gründen räumlich vom Hauptbaukörper getrennt. Die Anliefe-

Four intersecting volumes make up the technical ensemble of the building housing the workshop of Städtische Werke, Winterthur (CH), designed by the Zurich architect, Theo Hotz. The volume-related conception allows a gradual reaction to the variably formed cityscape with its individual design. In Zürcherstraße its entire dimension clearly appears as an industrial building whilst the rear part of the building, gradually moves down to the height of the planned residential buildings.

The separate parts of the building fulfil different functional requirements. The main body of the building contains the main workshop and vehicle hall. For climatic and operational reasons, the storage section is physically separated from the main body of the building. Deliveries arrive via the large vehicle hall.

CONSTRUCTEC-Preis 1996

**Betriebsgebäude Gaswerkareal – Städtische Werke: Ansicht; Detail/
Work shop centre: view; detail**

rung erfolgt durch die große Fahrzeughalle.

Büro- und Galeriewerkstättentrakt entsprechen den höchsten Anforderungen an den Ausbaustandard. Kurze Wege für die betrieblichen Abläufe, ein großes Maß an Flexibilität und große Transparenz für visuelle Arbeitskontakte charakterisieren das Konzept. Sowohl innen wie außen wurden wenige, dauerhafte wie zweckmäßige, wiederverwertbare wie unterhaltsarme Materialien eingesetzt.

Kommentar der Jury Um ein thermisch-visuell behagliches sowie energetisch sinnvolles Gesamtkonzept zu erreichen, hat der Architekt für das Betriebsgebäude der Städtischen Werke mit seinen Ingenieuren eine Reihe von Maßnahmen entwickelt:
○ Gliederung des Baukörpers in Temperaturzonen,
○ Gliederung von Arbeitsbereichen und Aufenthaltszonen bezüglich Ausblick, Tageslichteinfall, Sonneneinstrahlung,
○ differenzierte Fassadenkonzepte zu den einzelnen Himmelsrichtungen,
○ Dachgestaltung mit Oberlichtelementen,
○ Energie-Verbundsystem mit BHKW-Anlage zur Strom- und Wärmeerzeugung,
○ Kollektoranlage zur Brauchwarmwassererzeugung.

Die vorgenannten Maßnahmen bei allen drei Bauwerken sind hervorragende Beispiele ganzheitlicher Planungsansätze und integrierter Planung, die zu einer Minimierung des technischen Ausbaus bei gleichzeitiger Minimierung der Energiekosten führen. Die Fassaden sind dabei nicht nur hinsichtlich der Sichtbeziehungen, des Tageslichteinfalls, der Beschattung und Besonnung, sondern auch bezüglich der natürlichen Belüftung infolge Thermik oder Windanfall beispielhaft ausgebildet.

The office and galleried workshop sections fulfil the highest construction requirements. The concept is characterised by internal business routes, a high level of flexibility and transparency for visual professional contact. Neither internally nor externally only few materials being durable, effective, recyclable and of low maintenance were used.

Comments by the Jury In order to obtain an overall concept with thermic-visual comfort and energetic usefulness, the architect has developed in cooperation with his engineers, various measures to apply to the „Betriebsgebäude der Städtischen Werke":
○ dividing the building body into temperature zones,
○ dividing work areas and recreation zones according to views outside, incidence of daylight, sun radiation,
○ façade concepts differing according to individual sky directions,
○ designing the roof with skylight elements,
○ energy-compound-system with BHKW-plant for producing current and heat,
○ collector plant for producing warm water.

The above mentioned measures inherent in all three buildings are outstanding examples for uniform planning stages and integrated planning, leading towards minimizing the technical outfit and simultaneously with it the costs of energy consumption. The façades are exemplarily well formed not only with regard to visual inter-relationship, daylight incidence, overshadowing and sun radiation, but also in respect of natural ventilation caused by thermic or winds.

CONSTRUCTEC Prize 1996

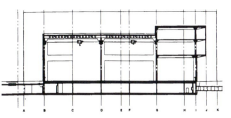

**Betriebsgebäude Gaswerkareal – Städtische Werke: Eingang; Querschnitt/
Work shop centre: entrance; cross section**

CONSTRUCTEC-Preis 1996

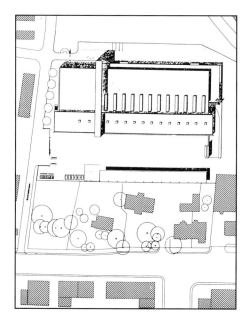

Betriebsgebäude Gaswerkareal – Städtische Werke: Lageplan; Grundrisse; Längsschnitt/ Work shop centre: site plan; floor plans; longitudinal section

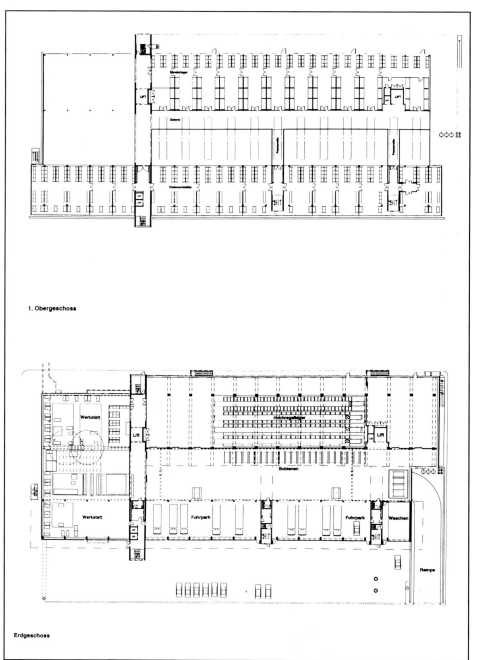

48

CONSTRUCTEC Prize 1996

**Betriebsgebäude Gaswerkareal – Städtische Werke: Ansichten; Detail/
Work shop centre: views; detail**

49

EMPA – Eidgenössische Materialprüf- und Forschungsanstalt, St. Gallen (CH)

CONSTRUCTEC Prize 1996

Klarheit und Dynamik kennzeichnen die Gestalt des Gebäudeensembles der Eidgenössischen Materialprüf- und Forschungsanstalt, das der Zürcher Architekt Theo Hotz in St. Gallen (CH) realisiert hat. Topografische Gegebenheiten und langfristig gewachsene Strukturen der benachbarten Bebauung wurden berücksichtigt. Durch die Plazierung des Neubaus an der südlichen Hangseite einer Senke zwischen dem Stadtkern und dem Dorf Bruggen wird der Freiraum zwischen den Siedlungsteilen erhalten. Der längliche Baukörper orientiert sich mit seinem Labor- und Forschungstrakt an der Richtung des Landschaftsraumes.

Drei unterschiedliche Volumen prägen die Gebäudestaffelung: östlich der lange, in sich gegliederte Labor- und Forschungstrakt mit dem vorgestellten Volumen des Labors der Fallprüfung; parallel dazu der niedrige Unterstand für den Werkhof; westlich der Straßentrennung der schmale Baukörper der Verwaltung. Dieser Trakt wird als „Kopf" des Ensembles und als Bezugspunkt bestehender und zukünftiger Bebauungen aufgefaßt. Horizontale Gebäudestrukturen und vertikale Elemente wie Treppentürme, Lifte und der Fallprüfturm stehen in spannungsreichem Kontrast. Die relativ großen Gebäudevolumen, strukturiert durch die vertikalen Elemente, fügen sich gut auf der Nordseite ein.

Die einfachen Gebäudestrukturen bestehen aus Stahlbeton-Decken und -Stützen. Die Fassaden werden durch eine tragende Struktur aus Stahl und aus minimierten, in der Fabrik vorgefertigten Aluminium- und Chromstahlelementen gebildet, die große Glasanteile haben. Alle Erschließungstürme werden durch rahmenlose, großflächige Verglasungen geprägt. PVC- und FCKW-haltige Materialien wurden konsequent gemieden.

Clarity and dynamics characterise the form of the building ensemble housing the Eidgenössische Materialprüf- und Forschungsanstalt, St. Gallen (CH) designed by the Zurich architect Theo Hotz. Topographic conditions and structures of existing neighbouring buildings, developed over many years were taken into consideration. The positioning of the new building on the southern slope of a valley situated between the city centre and the village of Bruggen allowed the preservation of the open space between the sections of the settlement. The elongated shape of the body of the building, comprising of the laboratory and research section, was adapted to the surrounding landscape.

Three contrasting volumes create a gradual effect of the building, i.e. to the east the long partitioned joint laboratory and research section with the volume housing the laboratory conducting gravitational tests; parallel to this the low shelter of the factory building and to the west of the separating road, the narrow building housing the administration. This section is considered as the "head" of the ensemble and the reference point for existing buildings and future constructions. The horizontal building design offers an impressive contrast with its vertical elements such as staircases, elevators and the gravitational test tower. The relatively large dimensions of the building, structured by the vertical elements, fit in well on the northern side.

The simplistic structure is made from reinforced concrete ceilings and supports. The façades are formed by the load-bearing structure consisting of steel and minimised prefabricated aluminium and chromium-steel elements containing large glass areas. All development towers are shaped by frameless extensive glazing. The use of PVC- and CFC-

EMPA – Eidgenössische Materialprüf- und Forschungsanstalt/Material research centre, St. Gallen (CH)

Bauherr/client:
Amt für Bundesbauten, Baukreis 4, Zürich/ Zurich (CH)
Architekt/architect:
Theo Hotz, Architekt BSA, Zürich/Zurich (CH)
Technische Gebäudeausrüstung/technical equipment:
Enplan, St. Gallen/ H. Keller, St. Gallen/ JBG, St. Gallen (CH)
Tragwerksplanung/structural engineering:
Fürer, Bergflödt, Köppel, Bauingenieure, St. Gallen (CH)
Fertigstellung/date of completion: 1996
Fotos: Markus Fischer (11)

51

EMPA – Eidgenössische Materialprüf- und Forschungsanstalt: Detail; Ansicht/ Material research centre: detail; view

Im Labortrakt wurden Photovoltaik-Zellen neuester Bauart, in transluzente Glaspaneele einlaminiert, vor den Fassaden montiert (flächenbündig und senkrecht gegenüber der Fassadenebene eingebaut). Beim Verwaltungstrakt sind die Paneele gegenüber der Fassade unter 75° schräg gestellt.

Kommentar der Jury   Wie bei den beiden anderen Objekten wurde auch beim EMPA-Gebäude in gleicher intelligenter Weise vorgegangen, um ein schlüssiges Gesamtkonzept zu erreichen. Differenzierte Fassadenausbildungen mit unterschiedlichen Fenstergrößen, unterschiedlichen Sonnenschutzelementen, Ausbaustandards, Speichermöglichkeiten, abgesetzten Betonstrukturen und gebäudetechnischen Ausbauten führen zu einer überzeugenden Gesamtlösung.

containing materials was avoided.

In the laboratory section the latest photoelectric cells were laminated into translucent glass panels and mounted on the front of the façade (flush and perpendicularly to the level of the façade). In the administrative section the panels are offset from the façade at an angle of 75°.

Comments by the Jury   As was the case with the above mentioned two projects, an equally intelligent procedure was applied in respect of the EMPA building in order to obtain a conclusive overall concept. Differentiated forming of the façades with varying window sizes, different sun protection elements, interior completion standards, storage places, shaped concrete structures, completions regarding the building technique convey the impression of a convincing solution overall.

**EMPA – Eidgenössische Materialprüf- und Forschungsanstalt: Fassaden mit Sonnenschutz; Licht im Innenraum/
Material research centre: façades with brises soleils; light in the interior**

CONSTRUCTEC-Preis 1996

EMPA – Eidgenössische Materialprüf- und Forschungsanstalt: Lageplan; Fassaden; Grundrisse/
Material research centre: site plan; façades; floor plans

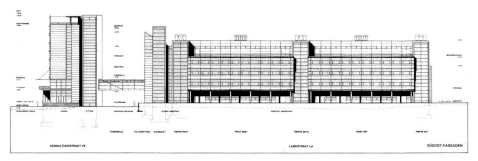

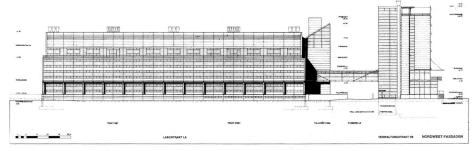

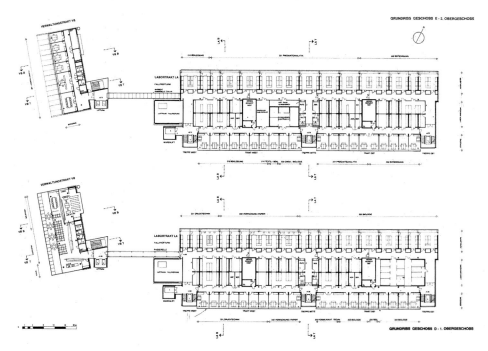

**EMPA – Eidgenössische Materialprüf- und Forschungsanstalt: Licht in den Innenräumen; Detail/
Material research centre: light in the interiors; detail**

CONSTRUCTEC-Preis 1996

EMPA – Eidgenössische Materialprüf- und Forschungsanstalt: Frontansicht/
Material research centre: front view

Für das Bauen in der Schweiz, dessen Thema in den letzten Jahren die Materialerkundung, die Recherche architecturale gewesen ist, demonstriert der Zürcher Architekt Theo Hotz, daß die entwickelte Technologie des Leichten, des Minimierten unvorhergesehen die Architektur von innen heraus neu definieren und verändern kann. Die These, das Material sei dazu da, den Bau zu bestimmen, aber der Bau sei im gleichen Maße dazu da zu zeigen, woraus er gemacht sei, war häufig auf das schwere, das undurchdringliche Material gemünzt: Beton. Theo Hotz gilt in der Schweiz dagegen als Glasbeherrscher und Freidenker (Benedikt Loderer), den die elegante Lösung fasziniert, weil sie zugleich die ökonomische, meist auch die intelligente ist.

For Swiss constructions whose theme throughout the last few years has been the detection of materials – Recherche architecturale – the Zurich architect Theo Hotz demonstrated that developments with lightweight material and minimisation can completely redefine and transform architecture in an unexpected manner. The theory, that material is used to determine the construction design and that at the same time the building served to demonstrate from which material it was constructed, was always based on the use of impenetrable, heavy concrete. Theo Hotz, however, is regarded as a glass expert and individual designer (Benedikt Loderer) in Switzerland, who is fascinated by the most elegant solution as it is also often the most economical and intelligent solution.

An der Transparenz der Gebäude ist nicht allein der Wille zur ästhetischen Lösung abzulesen, sondern der Erfahrungsprozeß der Optimierung im Materialeinsatz:

The transparency of the building reveals not only the desire for a pleasing aesthetic solution but also the experience in optimising the effectiveness of material use:

**Gebäude Lager-Technik/
Building store technology, Wolfurt (A)**

Die Einfachheit des Komplexen kennzeichnet das Gebäude für Lager-Technik, das die Vorarlberger Architekten Carlo Baumschlager und Dietmar Eberle in Wolfurt (A) realisiert haben. Vielschichtigkeit findet bei diesem gewerblichen Gebäude gestalterisch Raum: klare Struktur, stabilisierender Winkel mit massivem Treppenhauskern nach Norden, zur Straße, und nach Osten. Die Struktur des Gebäudes ist nach Süden und Westen transparent geöffnet und mehrschichtig gegliedert: mit freigestellten Fassaden, horizontalen Lamellen- und vertikalen Schiebeläden-Schirmen. Zur Straße, in einer transluzenten Hülle aus Gußglas verborgen: die Technik der Aufzugstürme des Parkhauses. Die Zonierung der Grundrisse bezeugt das Vordringen eines veränderten Entwurfsverständnisses in den Gewerbe- und Bürobau.

"Simplicity of the complex" characterises the building for storage technology, Wolfurt (A), designed by the Voralberg architects Carlo Baumschlager and Dietmar Eberle. Versatility finds creative expression in this commercial building through a clear structure, stabilising angles and a solid central stairwell built to the north, onto the street, and to the east. The sides of the building facing south and west are transparent, its structure consists of multiple layers, i.e. emerging façades, horizontal, venetian-style blinds and vertical sliding screens. Towards the road are the car park's elevator towers, their mechanics encased and concealed in translucent cast glass: The zoning of the outlines confirms the advancing changed design perception in the industrial and office building.

**Besondere Auszeichnung/
Special award:
ARGE Baumschlager & Eberle,
Lochau (A)**
Projekt/Project:
Gebäude Lager-Technik, Wolfurt/Vorarlberg (A)

Kommentar der Jury Der viergeschossige Betonbau beherbergt auf einem Stützenraster eine zweigeschossige Wartungs- und Montagehalle und zwei Bürogeschosse. Davor sind, zur Straßenseite, nach Art eines Hochregallagers in einer ganz mit Glas umkleideten, mechanischen Garage die PKW-Stellplätze des Betriebs untergebracht. Das Bauwerk wird zum Demonstrationsprojekt. Jede der vier unterschiedlichen Gebäudefronten reflektiert auf intelligente Weise ein eigenes Programm.

Nach Norden bildet der semi-transparente Glaskörper der „vertikalen Garage" die Straßen- und Eingangsfront. Nach Osten schirmt eine massive Betonwand mit nur wenigen Öffnungen den Lärm der benachbarten Autobahn ab. Nach Süden ist die Fassade raumhoch verglast. Externe Aluminium-Lamellen reflektieren das Tageslicht auf die Innenraumdecken. Die Westfassade schließlich artikuliert sich als tief geschichtetes Sichtbeton-Gerüst mit einem Achsabstand von 80 cm. Raumhohe hölzerne Schiebeläden fungieren hier als Sonnen- und Witterungsschutz.

Das Gebäudeinnere zeichnet sich durch kurze Wege, natürliche Belüftung und eine Ausstattung aus, welche sich auf das notwendigste beschränkt. Schaustück ist der 18 m hohe Glaskörper, welcher die drei vertikalen „Pkw-Regale" aufnimmt.

Mit ihrer unkonventionellen Lösung zur Bereitstellung ausreichender Parkplätze für die Mitarbeiter haben die Architekten zugleich auch ein Belegexemplar für „Pkw-Lagertechnik" im städtischen Kontext geliefert.

Der neue Firmensitz verkörpert ein Symbol der eigenen Leistungsfähigkeit, komplexe Produktions-, Wartungs- und Verwaltungsvorgänge mit einfachen Mitteln beherrschen und in eine ästhetisch wie strukturell anspruchsvolle Baugestalt überführen zu können.

Comments by the Jury The multi-storey concrete building, supported on a column grid pattern, contains a two-storey maintenance- and mounting-hall. Parking places for the company are provided for in a mechanical high-bay-warehouse-like garage cladded completely with glass and looking on to the street. The building has become a demonstration project. Each of the four different building fronts intelligently reflects its own programme.

To the north, the semi-transparent glass body of the "vertical garage" represents the street- and entrance front. To the east, a massive concrete wall with very few openings shields off the noise from the near-by highway. To the south, the façade is glazed room-high-wise. External aluminum slats reflect the daylight on to the interior ceilings. The west façade finally pronounces itself as a deeply coursed, fair-faced concrete scaffold with a unit spacing of 80 cms. Room-high wooden sash windows function here as sun and weather protection.

Special characteristic features of the interior of the building are its short ways, natural ventilation, and an equipment which is reduced to the absolutely necessary.

Show-piece is the 18 meter high glass body which comprises the three vertical "car-bays". Bay elevators carry the vehicles to a free space in the "glass box". By means of code-cards, a computer calls the cars back on request. With their unconventional solution for providing sufficient parking space for employees, the architects have simultaneously produced a spectacular example for "car-storing-technique" in an urban context.

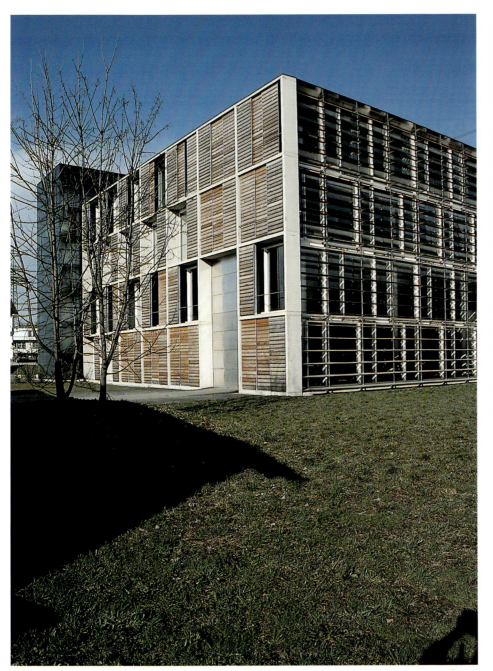

Gebäude Lager-Technik/Building Store-Technology, Wolfurt (A)

Bauherr/client:
Fa. Doppelmayr, Wolfurt (A)
Architekten/architects:
Carlo Baumschlager + Dietmar Eberle,
Architekten, Lochau (A)
Technische Gebäudeausrüstung/technical equipment:
Fa. Schlappach, Bregenz (A)
Tragwerksplanung/structural engineering:
Dipl.-Ing. E. Mader, Bregenz (A)
Fertigstellung/date of completion: 1994
Fotos: Eduard Hueber (6), Reinhart Wustlich (6)

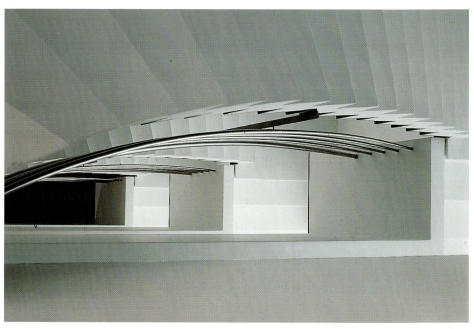

**Gebäude Lager-Technik: Detail Ostansicht; Treppenaufgang; Ostansicht/
Building Store-Technology: detail east elevation; staircase; east elevation**

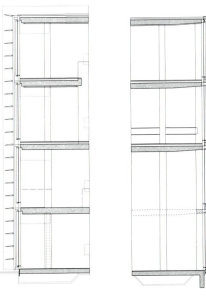

SÜDFASSADE   WESTFASSADE

**Gebäude Lager-Technik: Südansicht; Licht im Innenraum; Schnitt Südfassade – Schnitt Westfassade/
Building Store-Technology: south elevation; light in the interior; section of south façade – section of west façade**

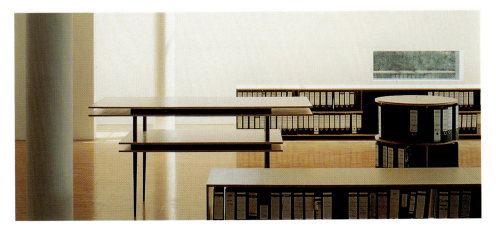

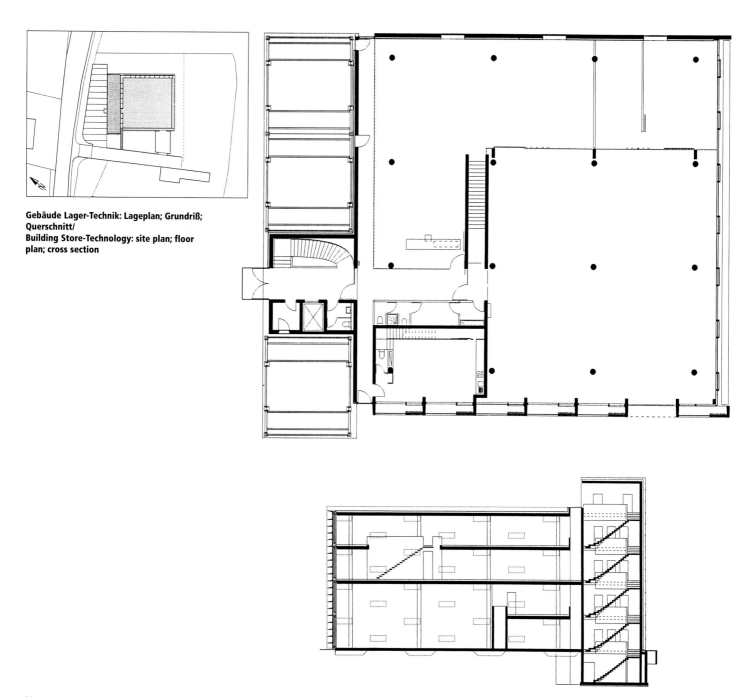

Gebäude Lager-Technik: Lageplan; Grundriß; Querschnitt/
Building Store-Technology: site plan; floor plan; cross section

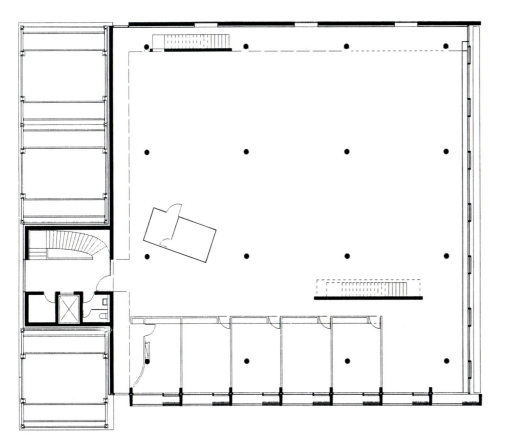
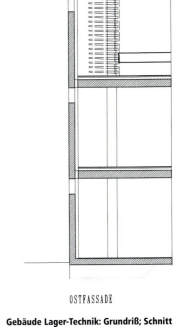

OSTFASSADE

Gebäude Lager-Technik: Grundriß; Schnitt Ostfassade; Süd-/ Westansicht/ Building Store-Technology: floor plan; section east façade; south-west elevation

**Gebäude Lager-Technik: Ostansicht/
Building Store-Technology: east elevation**

Moderne strukturelle Prinzipien und skulpturale Gliederungen gehen in der Architektur Carlo Baumschlagers und Dietmar Eberles eine Verbindung ein, die eine, regionale Grenzen weit übergreifende, Qualität bewirken. Die Unterschiedlichkeit der Progamm-Anforderungen, der Struktur- und Fassaden-Elemente zu zeigen, verhilft jedem Bereich des Gebäudes zu einem eigenen Ausdruck. Ihn zugleich zu einer Gesamtheit genauer Maßordnung, offener Transparenz und Übereinstimmung im Unterschied zu führen, zeugt von dem originären Status der Architekten. Die Akribie, die der Bestimmung und der Gestaltung von Gewerbehäusern gewidmet wird, sagt viel über den Willen einer Region aus, die Lebensbedingungen nicht mit Wegwerfprodukten des Bauens zu belasten.

The combination of modern structural principles and sculptural structuring in the architectural work of Carlo Baumschlager and Dietmar Eberle serves to achieve a quality level, transcending any regional borders by far. The variety of programme requirements, of structural and façade elements serve to give each part of the building its individual expression. Their ability to combine this to a total of precision, open translucency and compatibility despite the differences show the innovative approach of the architects. The meticulousness dedicated to the purpose and design of industrial buildings is representative for the belief of a region not to contaminate its living environments with architectural waste.

Uhrenfabrik Corum/Clock manufacturing Plant Corum, La Chaux-de-Fonds (CH)

Die Rückkehr der klarsten Form der Moderne in die Struktur der alten Stadt wird durch das Erweiterungsgebäude der Uhrenfabrik Corum symbolisiert, das Margrit Althammer und René Hochuli in La Chaux-de-Fonds (CH) realisiert haben. Präzision und Transparenz des Technischen, eingelagert in eine umhüllende Betonschale – das Produktions- und Ausstellungsgebäude steht für die Identität von Produkt und Arbeitswelt und für die Identität von Produkt und Architektur. Der theoretische Scheinkonflikt zwischen Masse und Transparenz wird dieser Architektur gegenüber ebenso als ideologischer kenntlich, wie der, daß es historische Reminiszenzen brauche, um in einem historisch gewachsenen Bedingungsfeld „zeitgenössisch" zu bauen. Offenheit zum öffentlichen Raum, Konzentration zur Landschaft – das Gebäude stellt Arbeitsbedingungen als nachvollziehbare zur Schau.

The return of the clearest modern form into the structure of the old town is symbolised by the extension of the Corum clock manufacturing plant in La Chaux-de-Fonds (CH), designed by Margrit Althammer and René Hochuli. Technical precision and transparency enclosed by a concrete shell – the production and exhibition building represents the identity of the product and working world as well as the identity of the product and architecture. The apparent theoretic conflict between mass and transparency is ideologically visible from this architecture as is the fact that historic reminiscence is required for the construction of "contemporary" buildings in a historically grown surrounding. Openness towards public space and concentration on the landscape – the building displays comprehensible working conditions.

**Besondere Auszeichnung/
Special award:
Dipl.-Ing. M. Althammer + Hochuli,
Zürich (CH)**
Projekt/Project:
Uhrenfabrik Corum, La Chaux-de-Fonds (CH)

**Uhrenfabrik Corum/Clock manufacturing plant
Corum, La Chaux-de-Fonds (CH)**

Bauherren/clients:
Ries, Bannwart + Co. S.A., La Chaux-de-Fonds (CH)
Architekten/architects:
Margrit Althammer + René Hochuli, Dipl. Architekten ETH SIA, Zürich/Zurich (CH)
Technische Gebäudeausrüstung/technical equipment:
Herbert Hediger Haustechnik, Zürich/Zurich (CH)
Tragwerksplanung/structural engineering:
GVH, A. Vaucher, La Chaux-de-Fonds (CH)
**Fertigstellung/date of completion: 1995
Fotos: Christian Kerez, Zürich/Zurich (13),
Guido Baselgia, Zürich/Zurich (1/1)**

Daß die Technologie das Gebäude zu inspirieren vermag, ist dem Bau sinnlich ablesbar. In der Dämmerung und bei Nacht werden die unteren Geschosse mit warmem Licht belebt, während die Produktionsbereiche vom präzisen Licht des Rationalen ausgeleuchtet bleiben. Material und Licht, die Themen der Recherche architecturale in der Schweiz, werden hier auf sehr eigenwillige Weise interpretiert.

Kommentar der Jury Das „Gehäuse" der Uhrenfabrik ist so ausgesucht zeitlos, wie man es sich für eine wertvolle Uhr nur vorstellen kann.

Das Gebäude schließt einen durch seitliche Altbauten begrenzten Hof talseitig ab. Die ganz verglaste Fassade zum Hof, die vom Ort aus zu sehen ist, gibt – in Analogie zum Glas der Uhr – den Blick frei auf die inneren öffentlichen Zonen des Gebäudes: die Ausstellungsgalerien und den Zugang zur Mittelzone, welche die mechanischen Werkstätten und Laborräume enthält.

Die zwei Geschosse der Mittelzone sind wie das „Uhrwerk" über die Gebäudehöhe verteilt. Sie erhalten Tageslicht über geätzte Glaswände von der öffentlichen Zone. Die dritte Zone talseitig nach Südosten enthält, in den „Gehäuseboden" eingebaut, die Arbeitsplätze der Uhrmacherateliers.

In die umfassende Beton-Außenwand zur Talseite ist eine Stahlskelett-Konstruktion mit individueller Raumhöhe für die Atelier-, die Werkstatt- und die Galeriezone gestellt. Die außen liegenden Arbeitsplätze erhalten individuell zu öffnende Fenster.

Die Uhrenfabrik ist durch die klare Form und das materialgerechte Detail ein bemerkenswertes Beispiel zeitloser Industriearchitektur.

The building offers the sensory perception that technology is capable of inspiring the building. At dusk and at night time, the lower floors are illuminated with warmer light, whilst the production areas remain illuminated by the precise light of the rational. Material and light – subject of the Recherché architecturale in Switzerland, are in this case interpreted in an unconventional manner.

Comments by the Jury The "casing" of the Clock Manufacturing Plant is an everlasting one and very much the same precious clocks are supposed to have.

With its front showing into a valley, the building forms the boundary of a courtyard surrounded by old buildings. The completely glazed façade showing into the courtyard, which can be seen from the village, gives a free view – comparable to the glass of a watch – into the interior public zones of the building: the exhibition galleries as well as the access to the central zone comprising workshops and laboratories.

Similar to the "clockwork", the two floors of the central zone are spread out over the height of the building. Daylight comes in through corroded glass walls from the public zone.

The all-embracing concrete exterior wall, showing into the valley, has a steel-skeleton-construction with individual room-height adapted to the zones of the studios, workshops and galeries. Work places outside the above zones have windows that can be opened individually.

The Clock Manufacturing Plant is a remarkable example of timeless industrial architecture thanks to its clear form and the right choice of material in detail.

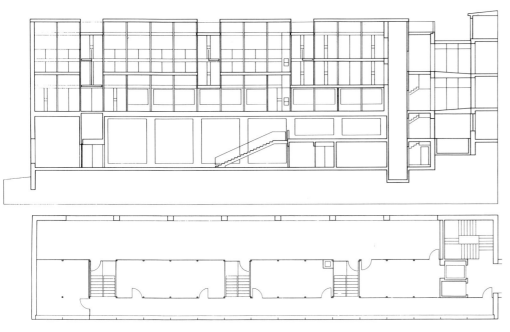
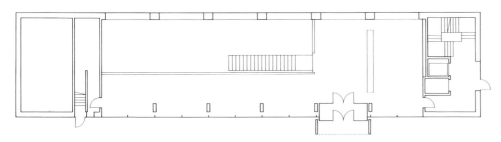
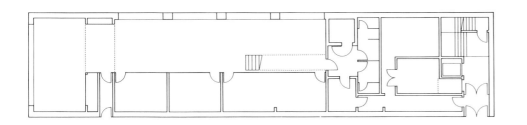

+8.60
+7.20

Uhrenfabrik Corum: Blick in die Werkstätten; Längsschnitt; Grundrisse/
Clock manufacturing plant: view to the workshops; longitudinal section; floor plans

Uhrenfabrik Corum: Flur der Werkstätten; „Medienfassade" zur Öffentlichkeit; Ansichten zum Hof/Clock manufacturing plant: floor of workshops; media-façade to the public (Foto: Guido Baselgia); views to the courtyard

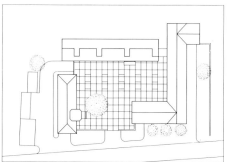

Uhrenfabrik Corum: Lageplan; Treppenaufgang der split-level-Geschosse; Empfangshalle/Clock manufacturing plant: site plan; stairs of the split-level-floors; reception hall

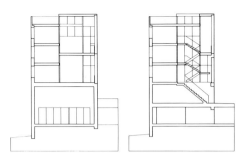

Uhrenfabrik Corum: Querschnitte; Ausstellung; Werkstätten/Clock manufacturing plant: cross sections; exhibition; workshops

Die Freude an der Präzision und an der Schlankheit des Querschnitts wird spürbar: das Gebäude dient nicht einem anonymen, austauschbaren Gebrauch. Nutzungs- und Funktionsschichten sind in drei „Folien" gegeneinandergesetzt, das Spiel der Komplexität wird mit split-level-Geschossen vor der breiten Glasfront gespielt. Das Signum der „Medien-Fassade" erhält keine künstliche Ausprägung: die Arbeitsprozesse selbst sind es, die wie im Schattenspiel abgebildet werden – Produktion und lebendige Teilhabe für die Stadt. Allenthalben hat die Suche nach Produktionsformen begonnen, die verträglich sind mit anderen Nutzungen der Stadt. Dies ist ein Modell, der Bau: prototypische Studie.

One can feel the liking for precision and slender cross-sections: the building does not serve an anonymous, exchangeable purpose. User and functional layers are offset against one another in three "films", the complexity game is played with split-level floors in front of the wide glass front. The symbol of the "media facade" contains no artificial stamp; the working processes themselves are displayed as in a play of shadows – production and lively participation for the town. Everywhere, the search for production forms, compatible with other uses of the town has commenced. This is a model, the building: a prototype study.

Uhrenfabrik Corum: Südostfassade/Clock manufacturing plant: south-east façade

SBB Stellwerk 4/SBB Signal Box 4, Auf dem Wolf, Basel (CH)

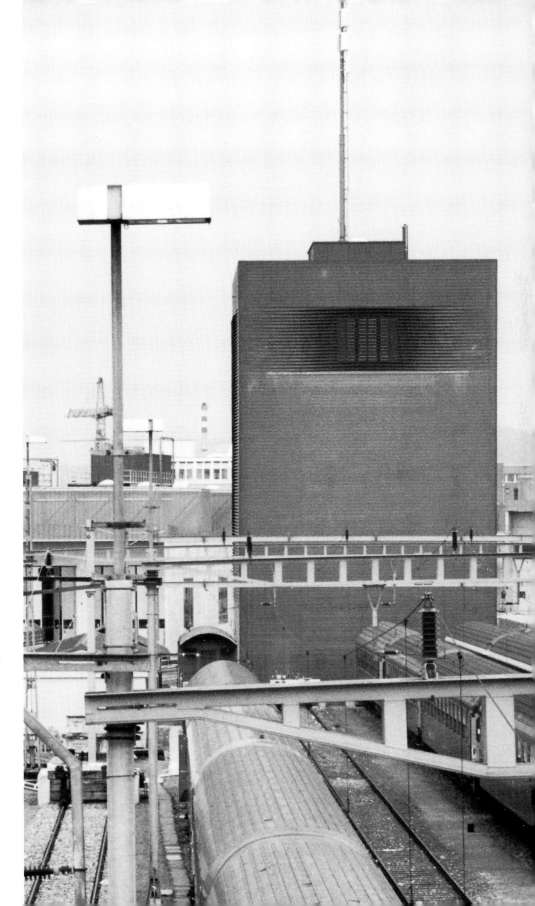

Massiver Kern und aufgefaltete Schichtung der Kupferhülle – das Thema des Stellwerks der SBB, das die Basler Architekten Herzog & de Meuron „Auf dem Wolf" in Basel realisiert haben: komplexes technisches Inneres und Gebäudekontur, die der Kategorie der Minimal art entsprechen würde. Die Doppel-Codierung der Fassade (physikalisch/ästhetisch) wird technisch mit Abschirmungserfordernissen der elektronischen Steuerungssysteme des Stellwerks begründet – mit der ästhetischen Paraphrase eines „Faradayschen Käfigs", wenngleich als solcher bereits die Stahlarmierung der Betonaußenwände funktioniert. Das vom sachten Richtungswechsel der Schnittkanten der Kupferbänder der Außenhaut (durch Verdrehen aufgestellt), von der minimalen Auffaltung bis zum strukturierten Licht- und Schattenspiel reichende optische Mikroklima des Gebäudes: ein Objekt.

Solid core and unfolded layering of a copper surround is the subject of the SBB signal box "Auf dem Wolf", Basel, created by the Basel architects Herzog & de Meuron: a complex interior and a building contour falling into the category of Minimal Art. The double coding of the façade (physically/aesthetically) is technically justified by the screening requirements of the electronic control systems of the signal box – using the aesthetics paraphrasing of a "Faraday cage" although the steel reinforcement of the outer concrete wall already fulfils this function. The façade of the building is created by the optical micro climate of the building, based on the slight directional change of the edges of the outer skin copper belts (erected by twisting) at the smallest opening, as well as the structural play of light and shadows.

**Besondere Auszeichnung/
Special award:
Herzog & de Meuron, Basel (CH)**
Projekt/Project:
SBB Stellwerk, Basel (CH)

SBB Stellwerk 4, Auf dem Wolf/SBB Signal Box 4, Auf dem Wolf, Basel (CH)

Bauherr/Client:
Schweizerische Bundesbahnen, Hochbau Kreis II
Architekten/architects:
Herzog & de Meuron, Architekten, Jacques Herzog, Pierre de Meuron, Harry Gugger, Basel (CH)
Technische Gebäudeausrüstung/technical equipment:
Fassade: Tecton AG, Pratteln; Selmoni AG, Basel; Sulzer Energieconsulting AG, Liestal; Balduin Weisser AG, Basel (CH)
Tragwerksplanung/structural engineering:
Proplan Ing. AG, Basel (CH)
Fertigstellung/date of completion: 1994
Fotos: Reinhart Wustlich

Geschlossenheit und Andeutung wird dadurch bewirkt, daß der Maßstab des Gebäudes im Gegensatz zu konventionellen Industriebauten „offen und unbestimmt" bleibt. Die Teilung der Geschosse läßt sich nur erahnen, die „Wicklung" drückt sehr bildhaft die physikalischen Eigenschaften der Hülle aus. Das Stellwerk ist Teil einer Erneuerungsmaßnahme der Bahninfrastruktur, zu der auch das unmittelbar benachbarte Lokdepot der SBB gehört, dessen Weichen und Signale wie die der anschließenden Geleise vom Stellwerk aus kontrolliert werden.

Kommentar der Jury Die Qualität des Projekts zeichnet sich durch die Art und Weise aus, mit der eine äußere Verkleidung eine einfache Beton-Box in ein Gebäude mit starker architektonischer Identität verwandelt, das als „Landmarke" an einer kaum näher zu beschreibenden industriellen Gleisfläche der Bahn steht.

Die Verkleidung, aus eng verlegten, horizontalen Kupferbändern bestehend, ist für das gesamte Gebäude als eine technische Lösung der Abschirmung für die elektronische Ausrüstung gewählt worden, die auf sechs Geschossen innerhalb des Gebäudes verteilt ist. Wo immer Fenster benötigt werden, ist die Verkleidung fächerförmig so aufgespreizt, daß es dem Personal möglich wird, hinauszusehen, ohne den Faraday'schen Käfig zu unterbrechen.

Die Auffächerungen geben dem Gebäude eine Leichtigkeit, die im Kontrast zur Masse des Gebäudes steht. Zugleich wird der industrielle Ausdruck bewahrt, der sowohl dem Programm als auch dem Ort dient. Die Wahl des Verkleidungsmaterials dient einer technischen und ästhetischen Lösung, von der zu erwarten ist, daß sie auch in Schönheit altern wird.

An effect of compactness and suggestion is created by the fact that the scale of the building remains "open and undefined" in contrast to conventional industrial buildings. One can only guess the position of the partition of individual floors, the "wrapping" vividly expresses the physical characteristics of the surround.

The signal box was part of the updating measures of the railway infrastructure, incorporating also the neighbouring SBB engine depot, whose points and signals and connecting tracks are controlled by the signal box.

Comments by the Jury The quality of the project is to be found in the way the exterior cladding has turned a simple concrete box into a building with strong architectural identity that stands as a landmark in a rather non descript industrial railroad area.

The cladding, made from narrow horizontal copper bands, has been used throughout the building as a technical solution to the protection of the electronic equipment located on six floors inside the building. Wherever windows are needed the cladding is transformed into lowers, that allow the personnel to look out while mainleaving the Faraday cage.

The lowers give to the building a delicacy that is contrasted with the mass of the building, while the industrial look, that suits both the programme and the site, is preserved. The choice of the overall cladding material provides a technical and aesthetical solution that is expected to age with beauty.

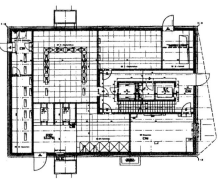
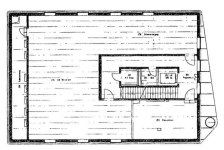

**SBB Stellwerk 4: Ansicht mit Lok-Depot;
Steuerungszentrale, Eingangsgeschoß/ SBB
Signal box 4: Elevation with coachhouse,
central floor, entrance floor**

Die „atmenden Flanken" des Stellwerks als biomorphe Zeichen – die Präsenz der verborgenen Masse der Gebäudestruktur bleibt spürbar, gerade weil die Organisation der Geschosse nicht ablesbar ist.

The "breathing sides" of the signal box as biomorphic symbol - the presence of the hidden mass of the building structure is still detectable, particularly as the organisation of the floors is not visible.

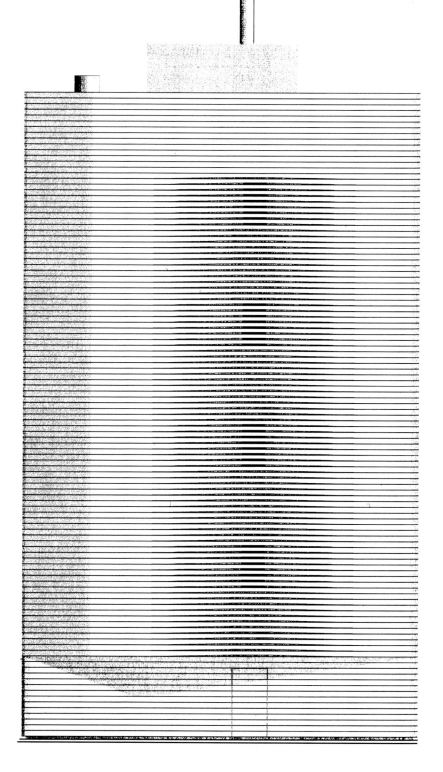

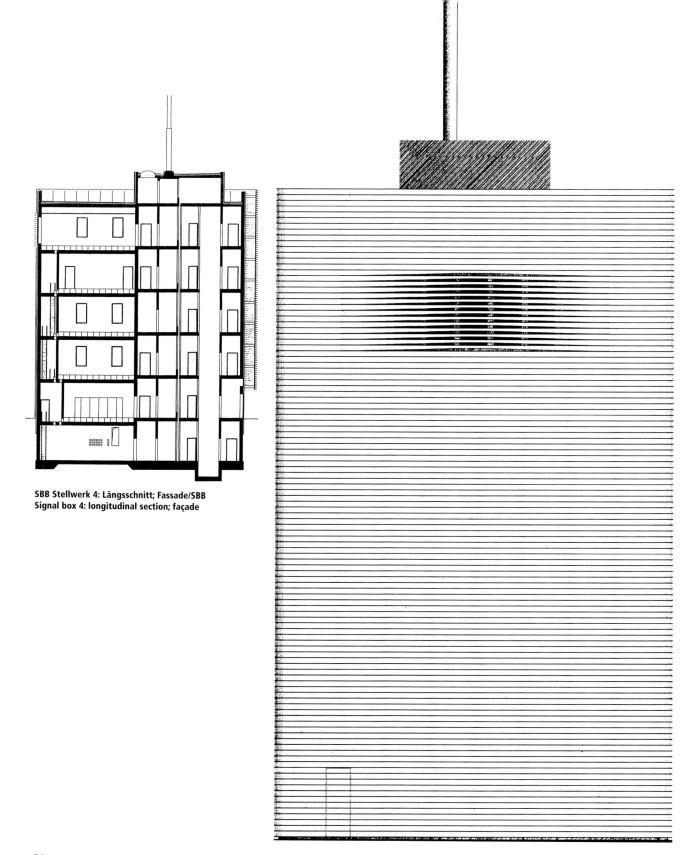

SBB Stellwerk 4: Längsschnitt; Fassade/SBB
Signal box 4: longitudinal section; façade

SBB Stellwerk 4: Gebäude in situ; Lok-Depot/SBB Signal box 4: building in situ; coachhouse

SBB Stellwerk 4: Fassadendetail/SBB Signal box: detail of the façade

Material: „Das Demonstrative, das in der österreichischen Architektur immer wieder auftaucht, ist uns zugegebenerweise sehr fremd: dieses Auskotzen, dieses Expressive" (Herzog & de Meuron – ARCH + 129/130 1995).

„Wir treiben das Material, das wir verwenden, an einen äußersten Punkt, an dem es von allen anderen Aufgaben als ‚zu sein' befreit ist" (Herzog & de Meuron, zit. in Martin Steinmann, Die Gegenwärtigkeit der Dinge – Mark Gilbert, Kevin Alter, Construction, Intention, Detail, Zürich-München-London 1994)

Material: "The demonstrative effect, constantly reappearing in Austrian architecture, is admittedly strange to us: this regurgitation, expressiveness" (Herzog & de Meuron – ARCH+ 129/130 1995).

"We utilise the material to the maximum effect so that it is released from all other tasks than 'simply being itself'" (Herzog & de Meuron, quote from Martin Steinmann, Die Gegenwärtigkeit der Dinge – Mark Gilbert, Kevin Alter, Construction, Intention, Detail, Zurich-Munich-London 1994)

Wasseraufbereitungsanlage der Sagep/Water purification plant of the Sagep, Ivry/Paris (F)

Ordnung und Zusammenfassung sind die Themen der Bearbeitung bei der Modernisierung der Infrastruktureinrichtung der Wasseraufbereitungsanlage der Sagep, die Dominique Perrault in Ivry realisiert hat. Sie versorgt einen großen Teil der Metropole Paris mit Trinkwasser.

Perrault nennt die Aufgabe eher „Verkleidung" eines technischen Prozesses als Entwurfsaufgabe. Dem Bauherren kam es darauf an, die neun Hektar große „Wasserfabrik" in den Seineauen möglichst unsichtbar zu halten. Die Herausforderung bestand eher darin, das architektonische Image im Zaum zu halten. Die Bedeutung der Anlage liegt in der Gestaltung einer auf sich bezogenen technischen Landschaft – und in der Schaffung der bestmöglichen Bedingungen für die Arbeitsplätze. Die Operation umfaßt zunächst und vor allem die topografische Setzung und Betonung – mit den Mitteln von Farbe und Licht.

Order and integration are themes for the modernisation of the infrastructure units of the Sagep water purification plant in Ivry, created by Dominique Perrault. The plant supplies potable water to a large part of the capital Paris. Perrault regards his task as more a "disguise" of a technical process than an actual design task. The customers were concerned to make the "water plant" – covering an area of nine hectares in the Seine valley – as invisible as possible. The challenge lay more in harnessing the architectural image. The significance of the plant lies in the creation of a self-related technical landscape and in the creation of the best work conditions. The operation comprised initially the topographical accentuation and emphasis – using colour and light.

**Besondere Auszeichnung/
Special award:
Dominique Perrault, Paris (F)**
Projekt/Project:
Water Purification Plant for Sagep, Paris (F)

**Wasseraufbereitungsanlage der Sagep/
Water purification plant of the Sagep, Paris (F)**

**Bauherr/client:
Sagep (Société anonyme de gestion des eaux de Paris)
Architekt/architect:
Dominique Perrault, Architekt, Paris (F)
Technische Gebäudeausrüstung/technical equipment:
Dogrement, Setec Foulquier
Tragwerksplanung/structural engineering:
O.T.V.
Fertigstellung/date of completion: 1993
Fotos: Michel Denancé, archipress, Paris (F)**

Das Labor- und Bürogebäude auf Stützen über den Wasserflächen und die Insel der „Rahmen" der technischen Systeme, einem enormen, transparenten „Luftkissenboot" ähnlich, das sich über den Becken erhebt, bilden die architektonischen Zeichen. Die Aluminiumfassade des emporgehobenen Gebäudes mit den horizontalen Öffnungen gleicht einer geometrischen Wabe. Die liegenden Zylinder aus Glas- und Metallelementen bilden zugleich die Begrenzung zur Stadt über dem Boulevard Jean-Jaurès. Hinter den gekurvten Gläsern, auf 200 Meter langen Fronten, liegen die Steuerungsanlagen. Die Zusammenfassung zu einem „technischen Garten" erlaubt es, auf eine 400 Meter lange Front am Flußufer zu verzichten. Einsame Zylinder seien entstanden, heißt es in Perraults lakonischer Anmerkung – und mit einer Spur mythologischer Überhöhung: ein Film-Set.

Kommentar der Jury Die Wasseraufbereitungsanlage zeigt beispielhaft die Integration eines großflächigen industriellen Projekts in ein städtisches Umfeld.

Im Kontext der zersplitterten Stadt-Landschaft werden die technischen Einrichtungen des Filterns und der Aufbereitung von Wasser bewußt zusammengefaßt und zu einer architektonisch gestalteten Großform gefügt. Die spannungsvolle Komposition von Bürogebäude und Technikbereich der Filter- und Aufbereitungsanlage gibt diesem großtechnischen Bauwerk eigene Bedeutung.

Die sinnfällige funktionale Ausbildung entspricht dem Anspruch auf Selbstverständlichkeit der technischen Infrastruktur im städtischen Kontext.

Die formal präzise Ausbildung ist dem Technikbau angemessen und erzeugt mit ihrer Ästhetik eine besondere Identität und die Möglichkeit zur Identifikation.

The laboratory and office buildings erected on supports over the water and the island of "frames" of technical systems, similar to an enormous, transparent "hovercraft" rising up over the basins, set the architectural features. The aluminium facade of the raised building with its horizontal openings resembles a geometric honeycomb. The horizontal glass and metal element cylinders form, at the same time, the boundary with the town via the Boulevard Jean-Jaurès. The control plants are situated on 200 m long fronts behind the curved glass. Due to the incorporation in a "technical garden" a 400 m long front along the river bank was avoided. Perrault laconically remarked that lonely cylinders had been created and, adding a touch of mythological excessiveness: nothing less than a film set.

Comments by the Jury The Water Purification Plant shows exemplarily the integration of a large-size project in urban surroundings.

Within the context of a dispersed city-landscape, the technical installations of the Filter- and Water Purification Plant are expressively put together so as to represent an architecturally designed large-size project. The composition, full of tension, of office buildings and technical areas of the Filter and Water Purification Plant attributes a specific significance to these large-size technical installations.

The meaningful functional form corresponds to the plant's right to be taken for granted plant in an urban context.

The formal precise shaping coincides with the construction and generates with its aesthetics a specific identity and an opportunity for identification.

Die Reflexion einer südlichen Landschaft – auch die Dimension der Infrastrukturanlage für die Millionenstadt kann mit architektonischen Mitteln dem Zustand des Un-Ortes entrissen werden.

The reflection of a southern landscape – the dimension of the infrastructure layout for the town can be saved by architectural means from a condition of nonentity.

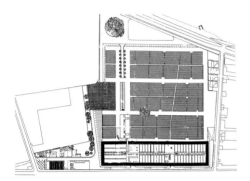

Wasseraufbereitungsanlage: Lageplan; Blick vom Bürogebäude/Water purification plant: site plan; view from the offices

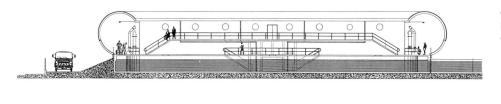
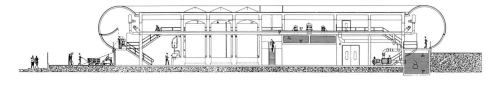

Wasseraufbereitungsanlage: Quer- und Längsschnitte/Water purification plant: cross and longitudinal sections

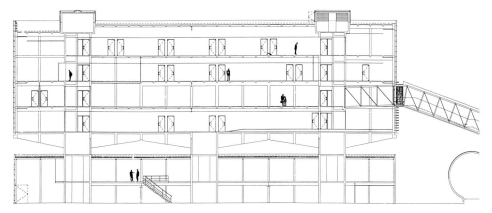
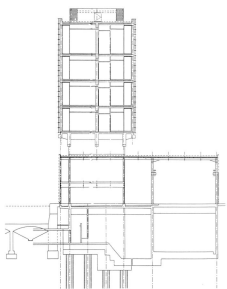

Die Glaszylinder um die Aggregate des technischen Prozesses der Filterung und Aufbereitung fassen witterungsgeschützte Arbeitsplätze zu einer erkennbaren Großform zusammen, die einem futuristischen „Luftkissenboot" gleich über den Wasserflächen schwebt. Der Riegel des Labor- und Bürotrakts ist mit einer Landungsbrücke dem Zugang verbunden.

The glass cylinders around the technical filtration and purification process aggregates combine weather-protected work places to a recognisable overall format hovering like a futuristic "hovercraft" over the water areas. The framework of the laboratory and office units is accessed via a gangway.

Wasseraufbereitungsanlage: Labor- und Bürogebäude/Water purification plant: laboratories and office block

Das „Luftkissenboot" des Rahmens der technischen Prozesse faßt die differenzierte Anlage geordnet und optisch beruhigt zusammen.

The "hovercraft" of the frame of the technical processes combines the different plant parts in an ordered and optically pleasing manner.

Wasseraufbereitungsanlage: Technische Decks, Labor- und Bürogebäude/Water purification plant: technical decks, laboratories and office block

Das architektonische Zeichen ist sinnbildlich für das Ziel des langen Prozesses, in dem Flußwasser durch Siebe, Vorfilter aus Sand, Filter und weitere Einrichtungen physikalisch, chemisch und biologisch soweit gereinigt wird, daß es „Qualität" bekommt. Der Prozeß wird durch eine gleichfalls komplexe Szenerie von Pumpen, technischen Aggregaten und Prozeßstufen begleitet, die eine industrielle Topografie, ähnlich dem Deck eines Supertankers, besiedeln. In diesem Fall kommt der Architektur selbst die Aufgabe der Ordnung und „Reinigung" des Prozesses zu – bis zu dem Punkt, an dem auch die Erscheinung des Ablaufes „Qualität" bekommt. Damit wird eine bedeutsame Aufgabe der Architektur geprägt: Gestaltfindung.

The architectural symbol represents the aim of the long process in which river water passing through sieves, sand prefilters, filters and other units is physically, chemically and biologically cleaned until it achieves a certain "quality". The process is accompanied by a similarly complex scenery of pumps, technical aggregates and process stages, covering an industrial topography not unlike the deck of a supertanker. In this case, the architecture itself has the task of ordering and "cleaning" the process – up to the point at which also the appearance of the discharge gains a certain "quality". This signifies an important task of the architecture: determining the form.

Zentrum zur Erforschung humaner Arzneimittel/Research centre human pharmaceutics, Leiden (NL)

Ein „Aggregat" der Architektur aus Schirmen und konstruktiven Strukturen ist mit dem Zentrum zur Erforschung humaner Arzneimittel entstanden, das die Architekten von CEPEZED in Leiden (NL) realisiert haben. Der gewerbliche Stockwerkstyp, ein Kubus mit seitlich vorgestellten Wind- und Sonnenschutzschirmen von technischer Ästhetik, begründet vielschichtige Innen- und Außenbeziehungen. Flexibel innerhalb des Konstruktionsrasters, linear erweiterbar innerhalb des durch die Schirme angedeuteten Volumens, bietet das Gebäude individuelle Arbeitsplätze in einem konzentrierten, stimulierenden Umfeld. Die Möglichkeit der Interaktion unter den individuell arbeitenden Forschern wird als besonders bedeutungsvoll beschrieben.

Die Erforschung der Auswirkungen von Medikamenten auf den Menschen ist für das Zentrum ein neuer, wachsender Aufgabenbereich.

The Research Centre for Human Pharmaceutics has been created as an architectural "aggregate" with screens and constructive structures by the architects of CEPEZED, Leiden (NL). The multi-storey office block – a cube with lateral wind and sun screens of technical aesthetics – represents multi-layer internal and external relations. The building, flexible within the construction grid and linearly extendible within the area indicated by the screens, offers individual work places in a concentrated, stimulating environment. The option of interaction between individually working researchers is described as especially significant.

The research of the effects of medicine on humans is a new growth area for the centre.

**Besondere Auszeichnung/
Special award:
CEPEZED/BV, Delft (NL)**
Projekt/Project:
Zentrum zur Erforschung humaner Arzneimittel, Leiden (NL)

Zentrum zur Erforschung humaner Arzneimittel/Research centre human pharmaceutics, Leiden (NL)

Bauherr/client:
C.H.G., Leiden (NL)
Architekten/architects:
CEPEZED/BV, Architekten, Delft (NL)
Technische Gebäudeausrüstung/technical equipment:
R. I. Boonstoppel, Nijmegen (NL)
Tragwerksplanung/structural engineering:
E.C.C.S./BV, Hoofddorp (NL)
Fertigstellung/date of completion: 1995
Fotos: CEPEZED

Eines der wichtigsten Ziele des Entwurfs bestand darin, die enormen Aufwendungen für Installationen zu reduzieren, die gewöhnlich für Gebäude mit medizinischen Einrichtungen vorgehalten werden. Die Bearbeitung dieses Ziels ist so wichtig für die Gewährleistung der Flexibilität der Nutzung und der Erweiterung – wie für das kleine Budget, das für die Realisierung zur Verfügung stand. In diesem Zusammenhang weist das Projekt nach, daß es nicht immer erforderlich ist, erhebliche Investitionen für die künstliche Klimatisierung aufzuwenden – ein generelles Ziel der Entwurfsstrategie bei CEPEZED: Reduzierung der Aufwärmung im Sommer – und Reduzierung der Auskühlung von außen im Winter.

Kommentar der Jury Das Projekt ist ein interessanter Beitrag für ein gewerbliches Laborgebäude, dessen Funktionen und endgültige Gebäudeausdehnung noch nicht völlig definiert sind. Deshalb sind Möglichkeiten zum Umbau und zur Erweiterung vorgesehen. Die Architekten haben diesem Problem auf intelligente Weise Rechnung getragen: Zwei weit über die eigentliche Hauslänge ausgreifende Schirme mit Lochblechverkleidungen begrenzen das Gebäude seitlich. Gehalten von regalartigen Stahlrohrgerüsten bilden sie den Rahmen, in dem sich das Gebäude künftig ausdehnen kann. Die Lochblechverkleidung läßt das Licht für die Fensterwände durch und bietet zusätzlich Windschutz und Verschattung.

Die Stahlkonstruktion des Gebäudes bildet eine leicht zu verändernde Baustruktur, die in den Details mit einfachen Mitteln klar durchgearbeitet ist. Es handelt sich insgesamt um einen sorgfältig durchdachten, architektonisch gut gestalteten, innovativen Beitrag zur gestellten Aufgabe eines Gewerbebaus für neue technologische Entwicklungen.

One of the most important aims of the design was to reduce the enormous cost of the installations normally required for buildings housing medical institutions. This goal was as important for guaranteeing the flexible use and extension as it was for the small budget available for the realisation. In this context, the project proves that considerable investments for an artificial air-conditioning are not always necessary – a general goal of the design strategy of CEPEZED: reduction of warming in summer and cooling from the outside during winter.

Comments by the Jury The project represents an interesting contribution to buildings used as commercial laboratories whose functions and final extension are not yet completely defined. To this end, provisions have been made for reconstruction and extension. The architects have given proof of their intelligence by taking this problem into consideration: two umbrellas reaching far beyond the actual length of the building with perforated plate cladding form the building's boundaries sidewise. Carried shelf-wise by tubular steel scaffolds, they form the frame for the building's future extension. The perforated plate cladding allows for the light passing through on to the window walls and offers additional wind protection and shadow.

The steel construction of the building is a structure that can easily be altered; its details have been clearly elaborated with simple means. As a whole, it is a carefully planned and architecturally well designed innovative contribution that answers to the given task of creating a commercial building for new technological developments.

Zentrum für Arzneimittelforschung: Flügel zur Gartenzone; Windschirme/Centre for drug research: wings to the garden; wind screens

Zentrum für Arzneimittelforschung: Erd- und Obergeschoß/Centre for drug research: ground floor, first floor

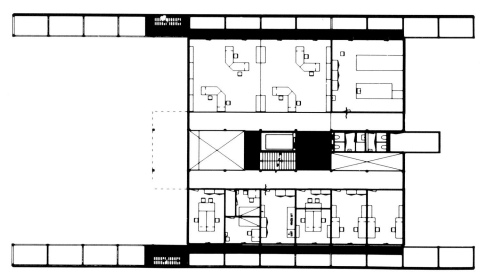

FIRST FLOOR

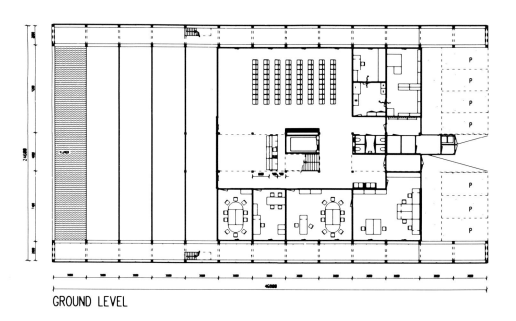

GROUND LEVEL

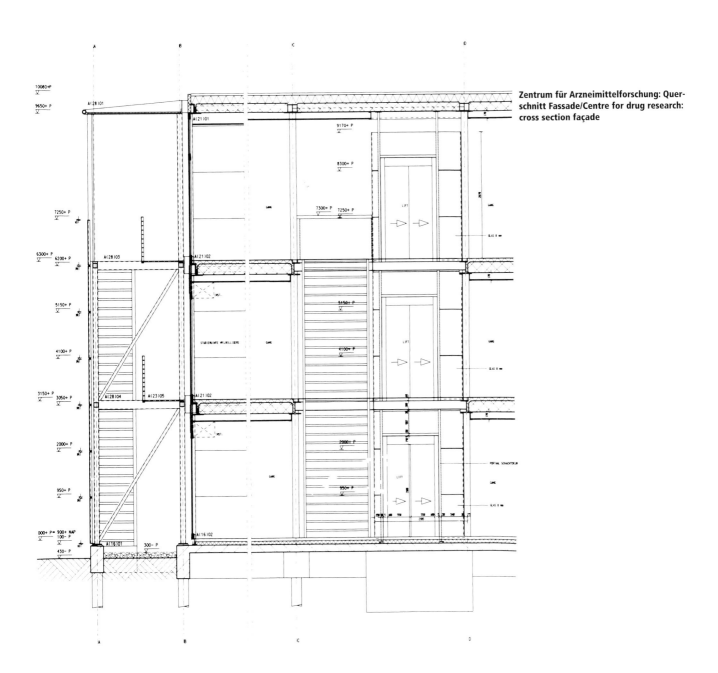

Zentrum für Arzneimittelforschung: Querschnitt Fassade/Centre for drug research: cross section façade

Zentrum für Arzneimittelforschung: Erdgeschoß; Fassadendetail; Gartenbereich; Innenansicht/Centre for drug research: ground floor; detail of the façade; garden area; interior view

Zentrum für Arzneimittelforschung: Schirme der Flügel/Centre of drug research: screens of the wings

Architektur mit Beschirmung: die Schirme dienen möglichen Anforderungen der Sicherheit, sie bilden visuelle wie gartenbegrenzende „Zäune". Sie reduzieren die Windgeschwindigkeit – die Fenster können geöffnet werden, ohne daß Unbequemlichkeiten durch Windzug entstehen. Die Windbrechung reduziert die Auskühlung der Fassaden und mildert den Winddruck im Winter. Als Sonnenschirme verbessern sie das Kleinklima im Umfeld des Gebäudes. Die Heizenergieverluste im Winter werden reduziert. Das räumliche Volumen wird differenziert: in das kompakte Gebäude und in ihm zugehörige Außenvolumen mit eigenem Charakter.

Architecture and screens: the screens conform with possible safety requirements, they form visual "fences" bordering the gardens. They reduce the wind speed – enabling windows to be opened without any unpleasant draughts. The wind breaking reduces the cooling off of the façade and reduces the wind pressure in winter. As sun screens they improve the surrounding of the building. Heating energy losses in winter are reduced. The spatial volume is differentiated: in the compact building and the respective external space of individual character.

IAM Institut für Angewandte Mikroelektronik, Erweiterung/Institute of Micro-Electronics, Braunschweig (D)

Als Gebäude für die produktionsorientierte Forschung und Entwicklung in der Anwendung der Mikroelektronik, das von den Architekten Schulitz + Partner in Braunschweig (D) realisiert worden ist, nimmt der Erweiterungsbau den bestehenden Kontext auf – und betont zugleich Eigenständigkeit. Technische Ästhetik und filigrane Schichtung bestimmen die Struktur des Gebäudes nach außen. Die Weiterentwicklung eines Bausystems aus den achtziger Jahren bezeugt Kontinuität und kreative Optimierung. Die klaren Hierarchien von Konstruktion und Ausbau, bereits in Systemzeichnungen aufgezeigt, bleiben am Gebäude sichtbar. Damit ist das Gebäude zugleich Beispiel des Wandels der technischen Auffassungen, der sich in Stufen vollzieht und an der Gebäudestruktur und -oberfläche ablesbar wird. Architektur als Feld der Rückübersetzung technischer Entwicklungen in das Entwerfen.

The extension to the building, housing the product-orientated R & D in the application of Microelectronics, designed by architects Schulitz + Partner, Braunschweig (D), absorbs the existing context and emphasises individuality at the same time. Technical aesthetics and filigrained layering, determine the external structure of the building. This further development of a construction system of the 1980's, shows continuity and creative optimisation. The defined hierarchies of design and implementation, already apparent from the system drawings, remain visible in the building. Consequently the building offers an example of the changes of technical perception, taking place in stages by reflecting these in the building structure and surface. Architecture as the field for retranslating technical development into the design function.

**Besondere Auszeichnung/
Special award:
Schultz und Partner, Braunschweig (D)**
Projekt/Project:
IAM Institut für Angewandte Mikroelektronik, Braunschweig (D)

IAM Institut für Angewandte Mikroelektronik, Erweiterung/Institute of micro electronics, Braunschweig (D)

Bauherren/clients:
Stadt Braunschweig, Land Niedersachsen, IAM
Architekten/architects:
Schulitz + Partner, Architekten BDA, Helmut C. Schulitz, Stefan Worbes, Braunschweig (D)
Technische Gebäudeausrüstung/technical equipment:
Ing. Büro Riechers, Ing. Büro Lindhorst
Tragwerksplanung/structural engineering:
Ing. Büro Harden
Fertigstellung/date of completion: 1994
Fotos: Schulitz + Partner

Die Aufgabe des Instituts besteht darin, Raum und Ausrüstung zu bieten für:
Testen von Maschinen und Produktionsabläufen (Ort: Maschinenhalle); Entwicklungsarbeiten für anwenderspezifische Schaltkreise, Sensoren und CAD (Ort: Labors); Fortbildung (Seminarräume, Hörsaal); Information, Ausstellung (Bibliothek, Zentralbereiche). Das Institut wird von einem Förderverein der niedersächsischen Industrie betrieben.

Der ursprüngliche Entwurf, der vorsah, den Baubestand pavillonartig nach Süden zu erweitern, konnte nicht realisiert werden, da einer Änderung der Bebauungsgrenzen im Bebauungsplan nicht stattgegeben wurde. Die Erweiterung wurde so auf zwei Baustellen auf der Ost- und Westseite vorgenommen, und hat zwei völlig unterschiedliche Gebäudeflügel zur Folge. Gleichzeitig mit der Gestaltung der Baukörperabmessungen wurde bis zu den Details eine Einheit mit dem Hauptbau des Instituts angestrebt. Eine lichte Atmosphäre der Arbeitsräume wurde erreicht.

Kommentar der Jury Das Institut bietet mittelständischen Firmen die Möglichkeit des Einstiegs und der firmenspezifischen Weiterentwicklung im Bereich der Mikroelektronik.

An den bestehenden Institutsbau von 1986 wurden funktional und gestalterisch sinnvoll zwei Anbauten gefügt, die in ihrer differenzierten Ausbildung der Fassaden einerseits den Bezug zum Bestand aufnehmen, andererseits aber auch ihre spätere Entstehung deutlich machen.

Eine konstruktiv präzise Ausbildung der Bauten mit konsequenter Schichtung der Fassadenelemente und ästhetisch wirksamer Präzision der Bauteile führt zu einem stimmigen Gesamteindruck mit qualitätvollen Innen- und Außenraumbezügen.

The institute has the task of offering room and equipment for:
Testing machines and production sequences (location: machine hall); development work for user-specific circuits, sensors and CAD (location: laboratory); teaching (seminar rooms, auditorium); information, exhibition (library, central areas). The institute is operated by a support association for the industry of Lower Saxony.

The original design, intending to extend the building to the southern side in form of a pavilion, could not be implemented as a change of the development boundaries in the development plan was refused. The extension was thus carried out at two sites on the eastern and western side, resulting in two completely different wings for the building. Simultaneous with the design of the building dimensions, the designers aimed for a detailed uniformity with the main building of the institute. A bright atmosphere of the working rooms was achieved.

Comments by the Jury The Institute offers to medium size companies involvement and company-specific continued education in the field of micro-electronics.

The Institute, built in 1986, was extended by two functional and well designed additions, which on the one hand are closely linked to the existing building by way of their fine façade forms, but on the other hand, give also clear proof of their later origin.

The precise construction form of the buildings, with its consequent layers of façade elements and aestheticaly effective precision of the construction parts, conveys a genuine impression overall with high-quality correspondences between inside and outside areas.

IAM Institut: Ansicht; Treppendetail/Institute of micro electronics: view; stairs detail

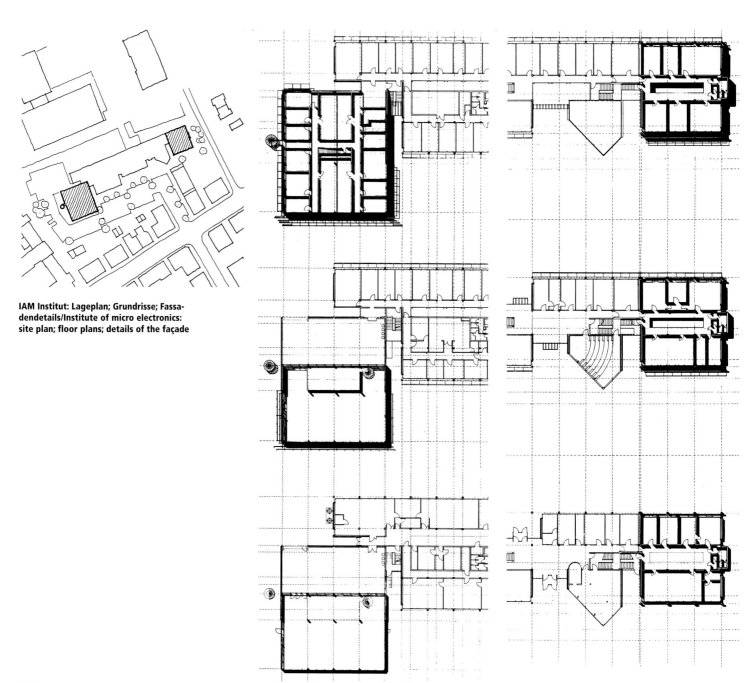

IAM Institut: Lageplan; Grundrisse; Fassadendetails/Institute of micro electronics: site plan; floor plans; details of the façade

IAM Institut: Fassadendetail; strukturelles System/Institute of micro electronics: detail of the façade; structural system

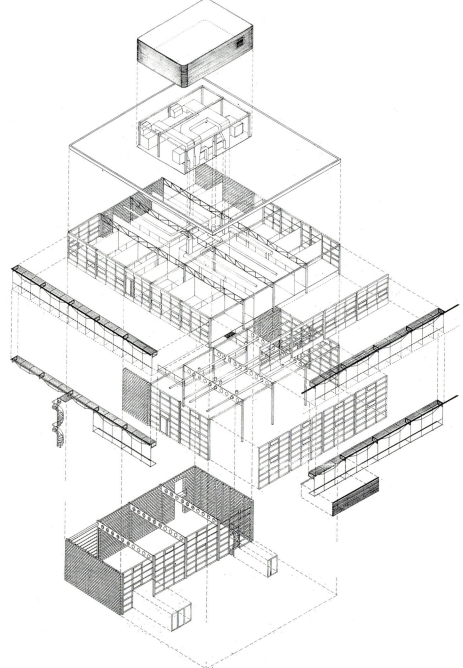

**IAM Institut: Ansicht; Fassadendetail/
Institute of micro electronics: view; detail of
the façade**

IAM Institut: Bürogeschoß/Institute of micro electronics: office floor

„Der neue Ostflügel nutzt die gleiche Rohbaukonstruktion aus Betonfertigteilen wie der bereits bestehende Hauptbau und ist auch in vielen Ausbaudetails identisch. Um aber ablesbar zu machen, daß es sich um einen acht Jahre später errichteten Neubau handelt, wurden einige Details und die Farbgebung bewußt geändert. Die nach außen sichtbaren Module der Naßräume mit Aluminiumblechverkleidung bilden mit ihrer Materialwahl einen Dialog zu dem ganz aus Stahl erstellten westlichen Anbau" (Schulitz + Partner).

"The new East wing uses the same shell construction of prefabricated concrete as the existing main building and shares many construction details. Some details and colouring were, however, deliberately changed to show that this was a new construction built eight years later. The externally visible modules of the wet rooms with aluminium panel cladding, form through their choice of material, a dialogue with the West wing extension constructed entirely from steel" (Schulitz + Partner).

Hallenneubau für ein Werkstattgebäude/Workshop A. & C. Wallner, Scheifling (A)

Übergreifende Struktur und skulpturale Elementierung kennzeichnen den Hallenneubau des Werkstattgebäudes für haustechnische Installationen, das der Grazer Architekt Andreas Ortner in Scheifling (A) realisiert hat. Unter gemeinsamen Dächern wurden mit offenen Strukturen die funktionalen Beziehungen des Werkstattgebäudes transparent gehalten, mit angedockten Metallcontainern ein lebendiges Ensemble der Durchdringung offener und geschlossener Bauteile begründet. Lager und Werkstätte stehen mit Verladung und Entsorgung in einem Ordnungszusammenhang. Die Aufenthaltsbereiche sind aus den Werkstattflächen durch eine Galerie herausgehoben. Die Architektur widersteht kompromißlos modern den Klischees einer Tourismusregion, die den Heimatstil fordern könnte, wie auch den Unzumutbarkeiten zeitgenössischer Gewerbegebiete. Architektur für ein Werkstattgebäude ist Architektur für ein Haus der Arbeit.

The new hall of the workshop building for technical domestic installations in Scheifling (A), designed by the Graz architect Andreas Ortner, features an encroaching structure and sculptural elementisation. Under mutual roofs the functional relations of the workshop were kept transparent by open structures, whilst connected metal containers establish a living ensemble of the penetration of open and closed components. Store and workshop form an ordered context with the loading and disposal areas. The recreational areas are formed as a gallery to separate them from the workshop areas. Without compromise, the architecture resists the clichés of a tourist region, possibly demanding a regional style, as well as the unreasonable contemporary industrial regions. Architecture for a workshop building is architecture for a house of work.

**Besondere Auszeichnung/
Special award:
Dipl.-Ing. Andreas Ortner, Graz (A)**
Projekt/Project:
Werkstattgebäude A. & C. Wallner, Scheifling (A)

Die Bedingungen der Arbeit ernstzunehmen, gehört zu den verantwortungsvollen Aufgaben des Bauens. Wenn heute europäische Regionen mit neuen Inhalten wahrgenommen werden, dann auch deshalb, weil sich in ihnen eine neue Art des Bauens für die Arbeit artikuliert hat.

Die Art des Gebäudes, in dem gearbeitet wird, kann zu einem Spiegel für die Art der Arbeit werden. Nicht nur Klarheit und Offenheit spielen dabei eine Rolle, sondern auch die Frage, ob Arbeitsplätze etwas mit der Darstellung der eigenen Arbeitsergebnisse zu tun haben, ob sie gleichmäßig belichtet und tageslichtnah konzipiert sind.

Kommentar der Jury Der Bauaufgabe eines Werkstattgebäudes für haustechnische Installationen wird durch die eigenständige Idee und sorgfältige Entwurfs- und Detailüberlegungen eine architektonische Durchbildung verliehen, die man sich bei Gewerbebauten häufiger wünschen würde. Dafür ist das Projekt beispielgebend.

Es wird anerkannt, daß die Gebäudecharakteristik mit ihrer Materialwahl der im Betrieb zu verarbeitenden Technik entspricht. Mit den überall klar ablesbaren, sauber gearbeiteten Konstruktionen werden Hinweise auf die Art und Qualität der handwerklichen Arbeit in diesem Hause gegeben.

Die Werkstattflächen sind grundsätzlich differenziert und nach Nutzungen aufgeteilt. Sehr gut belichtet versprechen sie eine gute Arbeitsatmosphäre.

Besonders erfreulich ist, daß mit dem leicht und transparent wirkenden Bau auf jede regionalistische Anbiederung an historisch überkommene Bauformen der Landschaft des Alpenraumes verzichtet wird.

Taking working conditions seriously is one of the responsible tasks of construction. If at present European regions with new contents are implemented, then this is also due to the fact that they express a new type of construction, geared to work.

The type of building in which work is carried out can be used to mirror the type of work. For this, not only clearness and openness are important but also the question whether work places influence the individual work results, whether they are evenly illuminated and designed with near daylight lighting.

Comments by the Jury The task to build a workshop for house-technique installations has been solved by way of independent ideas as well as careful design and consideration of the details, i.e. the building is filled with architecture, an exemplary solution one would wish to see more often with commercial projects.

It was appreciated that the characteristic features of the building and the choice of materials corresponded to those of the techniques applied in the workshop. The clearly visible and precise constructions that can be seen everywhere, draw attention to the type and quality of the manufacturing process carried out in this building.

With workshop areas being divided according to their utilization, the size of areas varies. They are extremely well lighted so as to allow good working atmosphere.

The Jury was pleased that the building, with its light and transparent effects, dispensed with any local familiarity towards traditionally historic building forms of the alpine landscape area.

**Werkstattgebäude A. und C. Wallner/
Workshop, Scheifling (A)**

Bauherren/clients:
A. und C. Wallner GmbH & Co KG
Architekt/architect:
Arch. Dipl.-Ing. Andreas Ortner, Graz (A)
Technische Gebäudeausrüstung/technical equipment:
eigener Betrieb
Tragwerksplanung/structural engineering:
Dipl.-Ing. Rüdiger Koberg
Fertigstellung/date of completion: 1994
Fotos: Ortner

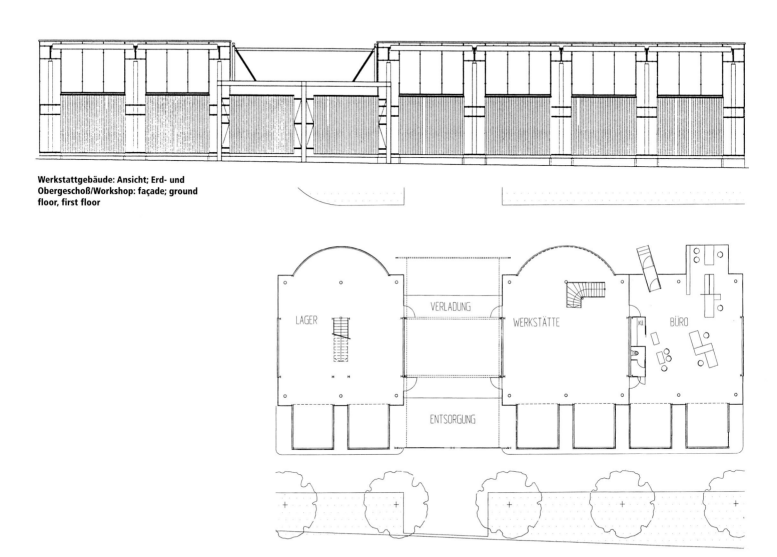

Werkstattgebäude: Ansicht; Erd- und Obergeschoß/Workshop: façade; ground floor, first floor

Die Herausforderung, die Rationalität des Komplexen einfach aufzubauen, durch Reduktion und Hinzufügung – und durch das Material, durch Glas und Metall, in eigener Qualität zu steigern, wird mit diesem Werkstattgebäude beantwortet. Die Themen Geschlossenheit und Transparenz werden mit technischen Mitteln bearbeitet.

This workshop building answers the challenge to simply construct the rationality of the complex by reduction and addition and to increase the individual quality of the material with glass and metal. The themes of uniformity and transparency are processed with technical means.

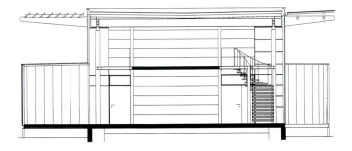 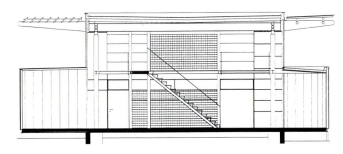

**Werkstattgebäude: Querschnitte;
Fassadendetail/Workshop: cross sections;
detail of the façade**

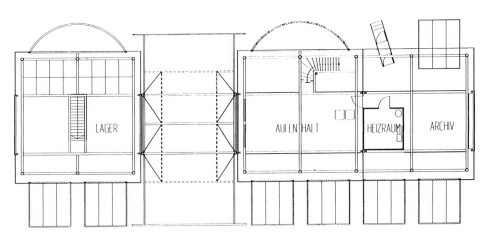

109

**Werkstattgebäude: Anlieferung, Entladung, Entsorgung/
Workshop: goods-in, loading, disposal**

Nachrangige Aufgaben des Werkstattgebäudes – Anlieferung, Verladung und Entsorgung – werden in das Gebäudekonzept integriert und ernstgenommen. Das Signal für den Arbeitsprozeß besteht darin, diese Aspekte der Arbeit gleichberechtigt einzubeziehen. Die Fragen der Sorgfalt, letztlich der Ressourcenschonung, spiegeln sich in dieser Haltung.

Moderne Technik und moderne Auffassungen von Konstruktion gehen eine Einheit ein: das Gebäude lernt von der Technologie und von ihrem Wandel.

Secondary tasks of the workshop building – goods-in, loading and disposal – are integrated into the building concept and given serious consideration. The signal for the working process is to equally incorporate these working aspects. The question of diligence and, in the end, the saving of resources, is reflected in this attitude.

Modern technology and modern design perception form a unity: the building learns from technology and its change.

**Werkstattgebäude: Ansichten; Innenraum/
Workshop: views; interior**

Werkstattgebäude: Teilansicht/Workshop: detail view

Die Industriegesellschaften haben, weniger bei den technologischen Vorzeigeprojekten als bei den eher nachrangigen gewerblichen Massenbebauungen, grundlegende Beziehungen zur Baukultur und zur Landschaftskultur verloren. Kreative Arbeit geht in trostlosen Gebäuden für die Arbeit unter.

Das Werkstattgebäude in Scheifling weist dagegen einen anderen Weg. So, wie der Betrieb seine eigene Arbeit ernstgenommen wissen will: sichtbare Installationen aller Art, die anschaulich die Arbeitsweise, die Perfektion der Verarbeiter wie des Materials dokumentieren – so nimmt er auch seine eigene Arbeitsumwelt ernst. Sie ist ihm wertvolles Gestaltungselement.

Industrial companies have, to a lesser extent in the technological flagship projects than in the secondary industrial mass constructions, lost the fundamental contact to the construction and landscape culture. Creative work has no chance in bleak work buildings.

The workshop building in Scheifling shows, on the other hand, another option. In the same way as the company regards its work as serious: all types of visual installations, showing the working method, the perfection of the operators and the material – it also takes its own working environment serious and regards it as a valuable creative element.

Inelcom S.A. Werk/Inelcom S.A. Plant, Valencia (E)

Das Werk für elektronische Ausrüstungen, das der Valencianer Architekt Arturo Sanz mit ACME Arquitectos (Carmel Gradolí Martínez, Luis Fco. Herrero García, Arturo Sanz Martínez) in Valencia (E) realisiert hat, zeigt gleichfalls eine Kombination aus Schirmen und konstruktiven Strukturen. Die Herstellung elektronischer Ausrüstungen erfordert ein klares, artifizielles Umfeld. Die Grundsatzentscheidung war, ein abstraktes Volumen zu bauen, das der Selbstbestätigung nach innen, inmitten der Unordnung des Umfelds, fähig ist – und das zugleich seinen Stand nach außen, innerhalb der antagonistischen Formen von „Ästhetik" in einem Industriegebiet zu behaupten weiß.

Als zweite Haut des Gebäudes wurde ein Schirm aus Aluminiumprofilen vor den Flächen der Außenwände des Gebäudes installiert, der die Fenster von außen schützt.

The works building for electronic equipment designed in Valencia (E) by the Valencia architect Arturo Sanz in cooperation with ACME Arquitectos (Carmel Gradoli Martinez, Luis Fco. Herrero Garcia, Arturo Sanz Martinez), also shows a combination of screens and constructive structures. The production of electronic equipment requires a clear, artificial environment. The principal aim was to construct an abstract volume, capable of internal self-confirmation in the midst of the surrounding disorder – and which at the same time could represent itself externally within the antagonistic "aesthetics" form in an industrial area.

The second skin of the building was constructed by an aluminium profile screen installed in front of the external wall areas of the building, protecting the windows on the outside.

**Besondere Auszeichnung/
Special award:
Arturo Sanz, ACME, Valencia (E)**
Projekt/Project:
Inelcom Werk, Valencia (E)

Inelcom Werk/Inelcom S.A. plant, Valencia (E)

Bauherr/client:
Inelcom S.A.
Architekten/architects:
Arturo Sanz, ACME Arquitectos (Carmel Gradoli Martinez, Luis Fco. Herrero Garcia, Arturo Sanz Martinez), Valencia (E)
Technische Gebäudeausrüstung/technical equipment:
Joaquin Solbes, Industrial engineering
Tragwerksplanung/structural engineering:
INCEC Engineering S.C.P.
**Fertigstellung/date of completion: 1995
Fotos: ACME**

Neue Nutzungen industrieller Räume – Laboratorien oder Werke für elektronische Geräte, schaffen eine Brücke zwischen traditionellen Typologien im Industriebau und Bürostrukturen. Zugleich kommt es zu neuen Beziehungen zwischen dienenden und zu versorgenden Räumen. Versorgte Räume großer Tiefe werden benötigt, die freibleiben von Hindernissen. Alle dienenden Elemente werden auf externe Positionen verwiesen. Die Grundrisse werden nach abgestuften Anforderungen zoniert: konditionierte und weniger konditionierte Räume (Klimatisierung und Überdruck).

Kommentar der Jury In den wohlbekannten Dschungeln internationaler Industrie-Areale ist es den Architekten gelungen, ihren Klienten vor der Außenwelt zu schützen. Zugleich entwickelten sie eine funktionale Arbeitswelt, welche die zeitgenössischen technischen Anforderungen aufnimmt.

Mit sehr einfachen Mitteln werden neue Lösungen für verschiedene Probleme gefunden. Die doppelte Haut der Fassade hat sowohl architektonische als auch technische Funktion. Indem an zwei Stellen die doppelte Fassade fehlt, werden Idee und Funktion dem Betrachter deutlich – im übrigen entspricht die Fassade ihrer Aufgabe, Licht und Blickbeziehungen zu filtern.

Eine logische, angenehme Arbeitsumgebung ist im Inneren entstanden. Sie ist geprägt durch gute Qualität der Belichtung und einen funktional klaren Zuschnitt der Aktivitäten.

Dieses Projekt zeigt, daß intelligente Problemlösungen oft zu befriedigenderen Ergebnissen führen als Architekturen, die nur auf formalen oder theoretischen Überlegungen basieren – und die in ihrem Umfeld untergehen.

New utilisation of industrial rooms – laboratories or workshops for electronic devices, create a bridge between traditional typologies in industrial construction and office structures, whilst at the same time new relations are formed between serving and serviced rooms. Serviced rooms of a large depth that stay free from obstacles are required. All serving elements were moved to external positions. The outlines were divided into zones according to graded requirements: conditioned and less conditioned rooms (air conditioning and overpressure).

Comments by the Jury In the well known jungle of the international industrial estates, the architects have succeeded in protecting their client from the outside world, and at the same time created a functional workspace that meets the technical demands of today.

With very simple means new solutions where found for various problems. The double skin of the façade performs architectonically as well as technically. By leaving the double skin away at two spots the idea and functioning becomes clear to the viewer, for the rest the façade does what it has to do, filter light and view.

A logical pleasent working environment is created inside with good lighting quality, and a clear functional split of activities.

This project shows again that intelligent solutions often lead to more results than architecture based purely on form or theory, that drowns in its surroundings.

**Inelcom Werk: Ansicht; Haupteingang/
Inelcom plant: view; main entrance**

Inelcom Werk: Ansicht von Norden, Südfassade/Inelcom plant: view from north, south elevation

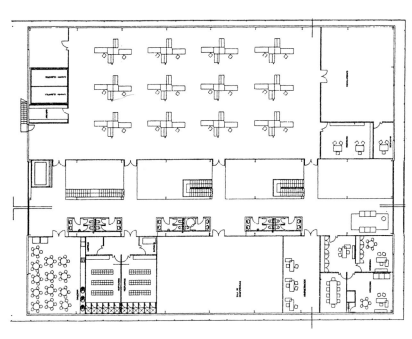

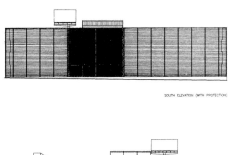

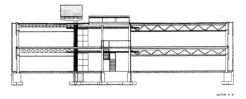

Inelcom Werk: Grundrisse; Schnitt/Inelcom plant: floor plans; section

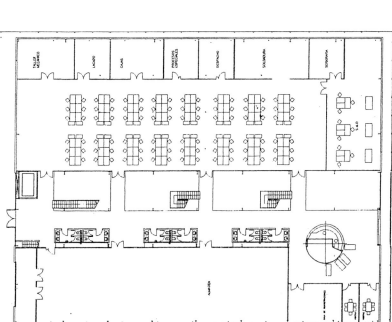

In Süd-Nord-Richtung besitzt das Gebäude eine offene Zone mit Eingangsfassade, Treppen- und Galeriebereichen und Nordlichtflächen. Die Nordfassade ist wegen geringerer Schutzerfordernisse nicht mit einem zweiten Schirm verkleidet, der Blick öffnet sich auf Weinberge.

In south/north direction the building contains an open zone, comprising an entrance façade, stair and gallery area and northern light areas. The northern façade does not contain a second screen due to the low protective requirement and thus offers views onto the vineyards.

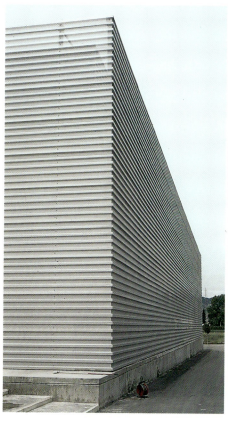

Inelcom Werk: Doppelte Fassade; Detail/
Inelcom plant: double façade; detail

Inelcom Werk: Innenraum/Inelcom plant: interior

Der Begriff „Technologie" wird unter Architekten schnell mit High-Tech übersetzt. Damit können sich Ausgrenzungen und Gegnerschaften bilden. Gleichwohl ist Technologie ein umfassender, ein prozeßorientierter Begriff, dem in aller Anonymität der komplette Wandel der Arten und Qualitäten des Materials und der Konstruktionsformen unterliegt. Die ausgezeichneten Gebäude des CONSTRUCTEC-Preises 1996 stehen als komplexe architektonische Zeichen für diesen Wandel. Als Beispiele der Technikgeschichte der Architektur zeigen sie nicht nur aufsehenerregende Entwicklungsformen, sondern vor allem: das in der Regel unbeobachtete Hervorkommen des Neuen, das der Wettbewerb erkennbar macht. Es verdeutlicht die Rolle, die Architekten beim Technologiewandel der Gesellschaft spielen.

The term "technology" is often translated as high-tech amongst architects. This can lead to exclusions and antagonism. At the same time technology is a comprehensive, process-orientated term, anonymously incorporating the complete change of type and quality of the material and construction forms. The buildings awarded with the CONSTRUCTEC Prize 1996 represent complex architectural symbols for this change. As an example of the technical history of architecture, they do not only show sensational forms of development, but most of all: the normally unobserved appearance of the new, that distinguishes the competition. This highlights the role, architects play in the technological change of society.

CONSTRUCTEC-Preis 1996

Die Jury des CONSTRUCTEC-Preises 1996 (von links nach rechts): Prof. Dipl.-Ing. Frank Werner, Münster, Dipl.-Ing. Dörte Gatermann, Köln, Mels Crouwel, Amsterdam, Sepp D. Heckmann, Hannover, Prof. Dr. Thomas Herzog, München, Dipl.-Ing. Andreas Gottlieb Hempel, München, Prof. Dipl.-Ing. Klaus Daniels, München, Dipl.-Arch. Jesper Gottlieb, Hellerup, Prof. Dipl.-Ing. Bernd Steigerwald, Potsdam und Dr. Ing. Reinhart Wustlich, Hennef (Fachliche Leitung).

Foto: DEUTSCHE MESSE AG, Hannover

TECHNIK UND ARBEIT – EINE EPISODE

TECHNOLOGY AND WORK – AN EPISODE

Eine Transformation der Wirtschaftsstruktur ist nicht so schnell zu bewerkstelligen wie der Paradigmenwechsel bei Leitprojekten der Architektur. Transformation der Wirtschaftsstruktur heißt, daß im Dienstleistungssektor ein Nachholbedarf in den industriellen Regionen besteht, daß die Transformation der Produktionsstruktur aber ohne die Einrichtung neuer Arbeitsplätze in den produzierender Sektoren nicht auskommt – wenn die Reduzierung des Arbeitsmarktes kompensiert werden soll. Das Projekt des gläsernen Hallenraumes der Akademie in Herne ist dafür exemplarisches Fallbeispiel. Im Beitrag über den Strukturwandel des Ruhrgebiets war davon die Rede. Im Sommer ist ein Großteil des Glashauses zum umgebenden Park zu öffnen, Sonnenschutzflächen, natürliche Luftströmungen und Wasserspiele tragen zur Kühlung des Ensembles bei. Eine optische und ästhetische Korrespondenz zwischen Parklandschaft und inneren Gärten, zwischen übergreifender Hülle, halböffentlichen Freiräumen und schützenden Einbauten entwickelt sich. Die Riegel der Einbauten bergen mit Wohnbereichen für die Teilnehmer der Akademie, mit Tagungseinrichtungen, Casino- und Freizeitbereichen und Verwaltung alle Komponenten, die eine Akademie benötigt.

Energie- und Klimaüberlegungen werden so kreativ in den baulichen Typus und in die gestalterische Form dieser vielschichtigen Anlage übersetzt, daß ein anderes Paradigma von Architektur entsteht. „Der Wettbewerb zog beinahe zwingend die Frage nach sich: Wenn schon eine so große Glas-Superstruktur, weshalb dann nicht gleich ein ganzes Photovoltaik-Kraftwerk? Inzwischen ist dieses Kraftwerk beschlossene Sache. Mit einer installierten Leistung von mehr als einem Megawatt wird es das größte gebäudeintegrierte Kraftwerk der

A transformation in the structure of the economy cannot be brought about as quickly as the change in paradigms in the leading architectural project. A transformation in the structure of the economy means that there is latent, pent-up demand in the service sector in industrial regions, but that the transformation of the production structure cannot succeed without the creation of new jobs in the productive sector – if the reduction of the labour market is to be compensated for. The project of the glass hall of the Herne Academy is an exemplary case-history. Concerning the part of structural change of the Ruhr this case is shown. In the summer a large part of the glass-house is open to the surrounding park, and sun-screens, natural air currents, and water-organs contribute to keeping the whole complex cool. An optical and aesthetic correspondence is developing between the park landscape and the internal gardens, between arching glass shells, half-public open areas, and protective interior structures. The lines of interior structures, with living accommodation for those attending the Academy, conference facilities, a canteen, and leisure areas, hold all the components that an academy needs.

Considerations of energy and climate are thus translated into the architectural type of this multi-layered complex so creatively that a different paradigm of architecture arises. "The competition almost mandatorily raised the question: if it is possible to have one so enormous glass superstructure, why not include a complete photo-voltaic power station as well? The decision has now been taken to include this power station. With an installed capacity of more than 1 MW, it will be the biggest power station in the world to have been integrated into a building" (Karl Ganser). "With the production capacity that existed at the time," Karl

Welt sein" (Karl Ganser). „Bei der derzeitigen Produktionskapazität", berichtet Karl Ganser, „hätte es zwei Jahre gedauert, um die notwendige Menge der Photovoltaik-Elemente, in Glas eingegossen, zu produzieren. Der Großauftrag schuf die Grundlage für eine Erweiterung der Produktionskapazität, was bei erhöhter Produktivität zu einer spürbaren Senkung des Stückkostenpreises führt. Der Auftrag geht an ein in Photovoltaik erfahrenes Unternehmen in Gelsenkirchen. Das Projekt in Herne stiftet also einen nicht unwesentlichen Innovationsbeitrag zum Aufbau eines Photovoltaik-Zentrums mitten im Revier". Das sollte etwas mit der Schaffung von Arbeitsplätzen im produktiven Sektor zu tun haben. Architekturpolitik könnte sich dafür einsetzen, daß vergleichbar unerkannte Ressourcen erschlossen werden.

Ganser reports, "it would have taken two years to produce the necessary quantity of photo-voltaic elements which are moulded into the glass. This major order created the basis for an expansion of production capacity, which raised productivity and led to a perceptible reduction in unit prices. The order is going to a Gelsenkirchen company with plenty of experience in photo-voltaic installations. The project in Herne is thus creating a substantial innovative contribution to the creation of a photo-voltaic centre in the middle of the Ruhr." This is supposed to have something to do with the creation of jobs in the productive sector. The proponents of architectural politics can strive for the opening up of equally unsuspected resources.

PYRODUR®

PYROSTOP®

Brandschutz

von

seiner

schönsten

Seite

Licht, Sicht und Brandschutz: Großzügige Trennwandsysteme für die G- und F-Klasse sind mit PYRODUR und PYROSTOP problemlos realisierbar.

Brandschutz und Ästhetik in Einklang

Ob Türen, Trennwände, Fassaden oder Dächer – wenn der Brandschutz mit im Spiel ist, brauchen Sie auf Transparenz längst nicht mehr zu verzichten. Dafür sorgen PYRODUR® und PYROSTOP®, die bewährten Brandschutzgläser der FLACHGLAS AG für die G- und F-Klasse. Ihre bauliche und brandschutztechnische Anwendungsvielfalt wird noch erweitert durch attraktive Kombinationsmöglichkeiten mit anderen Funktionsgläsern aus unserem Hause.

Als Pionier und Marktführer bei F-Verglasungen liegt uns viel daran, Architekten und Planern ausgereifte Systemlösungen zu bieten. So finden Sie PYRODUR® und PYROSTOP® Verglasungen heute in weit über einhundert bauaufsichtlich zugelassenen Systemen aus Aluminium, Stahl, Stahl/Aluminium, Holz und Beton. Das schafft Gestaltungsfreiheit und Planungssicherheit bei der effektvollen Umsetzung transparenter Brandschutzkonzepte.

Betrachten Sie den Brandschutz ruhig von seiner schönsten Seite – das Know-how der FLACHGLAS AG und ihrer Systempartner ermöglicht es Ihnen.

Brandschutz im Überkopfbereich: Unter den zahlreichen Systemzulassungen mit PYRODUR und PYROSTOP finden Sie auch Lösungen für Dach- und Schrägverglasungen.

PILKINGTON
FLACHGLAS AG

Ausführliche Informationen und Planungsunterlagen zum transparenten baulichen Brandschutz erhalten Sie über die:

FLACHGLAS AG
Haydnstraße 19
45884 Gelsenkirchen
Tel.: 0209/168-0
Fax.: 0209/168-2053

Brandschutz für Fluchtwege, Treppenräume und Brandabschnitte: T 30 und T 90 Türen mit PYROSTOP stehen in zahlreichen Ausbildungsvarianten zur Verfügung.

Atemtechnik

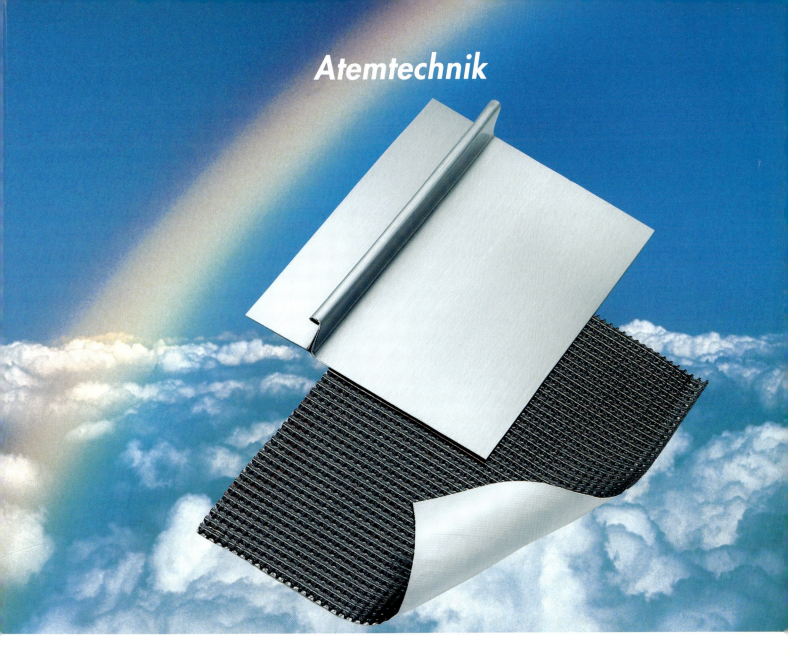

'Top-Drain' – die Gitter-Idee für Vollsparrendämmung.

Klöber bietet die Lösung für eine Vollsparrendämmung bei Metalldächern mit der 2-Komponenten-Idee 'Top-Drain', eine Kombination aus der extrem diffusionsoffenen Schalungsbahn 'Tyvek®' HD-Dry und einem Abstands-/Drainagegitter (Sd ≈ 0,03 m). Speziell konstruierte Gitterkanäle sorgen für zuverlässigen Abtransport der Feuchtigkeit und ermöglichen die Belüftung zwischen der diffusionsoffenen Trennlage und der Metalleindeckung. 'Top-Drain' wird auf der Schalung paralell zum Ortgang verlegt und der Überdeckungsbereich mit Klöber 'Butylon' geschlossen.

®'Tyvek' ist ein eingetragenes Warenzeichen für Polyolefinspinnvlies von Du Pont.

Klöber GmbH & Co. KG
Scharpenberger Str. 72-90
58256 Ennepetal
Telefon 0 23 33/ 98 77- 0
Telefax 0 23 33/ 98 77-199

Besuchen Sie uns in
Halle 5, Stand B 18

Für Europas Dächer.